THE CAMROSE SCANDAL

By

DAVID GRAHAM

To the long-suffering football fraternity in Basingstoke.
The largest town in the country without a football league side.

CONTENTS

ACKNOWLEDGMENTS

David Partridge
Julie Partridge
Graham Merry – Basingstoke Gazette
Katie French – Basingstoke Gazette Editor
Basingstoke Gazette = Staff
Stuart Graham
Matthew Graham
Steve Frangou
Adrian Donnelly
Colin Stoker
Basingstoke Town ex-footballers
Luke and Elayne Mullen - Hartley Wintney Football Club
Josie Shipman - Photographer
Basingstoke Town FC ex-footballers group
Basingstoke Council staff
Kim Hawker and Basingstoke Discovery Centre staff

PREFACE

This book is about the efforts of a group of protesters determined to prevent the Development for housing on the local football ground.

The Camrose Scandal will probably be remembered as one of the worst ever in Non League football. Basingstoke Town football club were on the low cycle of their cash flow. One of the sponsors was a company called CENTERPRISE and their owner was Rafi Razzak a multi-millionaire. As a sponsor he was warmly welcomed and managed to gain access to a leading role within the club. With the help of the CENTERPRISE sponsorship the club had a halcyon period in the late 1990s which included a ground record attendance. However the club carried a debt from times past and at the turn of the century a sizable debt was announced. The club turned to the CENTERPRISE owner for help and as they say the rest is history.

The sad thing about this scandal is the length of time it has gone on. Since Rafi Razzak took over the team has dropped down from the Conference South league (Level B) to the Southern League South West Division (Level D). Even worse the ground has been degraded by the owner who eventually finished up destroying it. Where Basingstoke Town could rub shoulders with Woking, Eastleigh and Farnborough who have all got good venue's they are now homeless. The club is currently ground sharing at Winchester City.

Added into the tale of woe Basingstoke has an extremely weak local council. Few of the Councillors appear to have much interest in Sport let alone football. The Camrose Scandal has virtually washed over them. Above them the Basingstoke Council Executive appears to be a totally unaccountable group who receive huge pay-offs and

1

pension contributions. This is often highlighted by the local newspapers the Basingstoke Gazette and the Basingstoke Observer. Basingstoke Council were granted a Covenant from Lord Camrose for 100 years which was due to end in 2053. To most people's astonishment the Council claimed that the Covenant was 'lost' when the Protesters were trying to save the ground.

BasingstokeTown football club are definitely the biggest of the sleeping giants in the Football Association Pyramid. The town is the largest in England without a Football League team. The potential for the town is there and the right decisions will see the club reach its potential. This will bring business to the borough and inspire the various football groups to get involved. A top class professional match day will be experienced providing enjoyment to similar levels as experienced at the Anvil.

This book traces the many twists and turns to reach the present situation which although encouraging is far from resolved as I write in June 2020. I hope you will enjoy the book and we sincerely hope to see Basingstoke Town Football Club in their own ground in the not too distant future.

David Graham

2020

CHAPTER 1

A WEEK IN POLITICS

MARIA MILLER MP

Summer 2019 had come along and for the first time in my life I decided to have a week in politics. No issue could have roused me thus far to get involved but this one was annoying me and something had to be done. The issue was the Camrose Scandal, surely the biggest scandal ever in non-league football.

First port of call was to e-mail the three local Councillors in my ward. Hayley Eachus, Tony Capon and Anne Court were the names to contact alongside their smiling faces and details on the Basingstoke and Deane Borough Council website. First up, Hayley Eachus and a bad start was that her e-mail box was out of action. I left phone messages but no reply was forthcoming. Next up, Tony Capon and a success in that his e-mail box seemed to work. Alas, no reply was forthcoming. Could it be third time lucky? I contacted Ann Court whose name I recognised from the Kempshott circulars. 'Success' – I got a reply!! Ann was helpful and gave me the contact at the Council: Steph Condon, who was dealing with issues related to the Camrose. Ann advised that the Council leader Ken Rhatagan was the person dealing with the Camrose issue.

So it was up to Ken to try and get some help. A few pleasant e-mails were exchanged before things came to end with Ken indicating he did not want to deal with me on the Camrose Scandal. The four Councillor names thus far were all members of the Conservative Party. The Tories dominate Basingstoke in the political arena. Most of the time they seem to control outright with the majority of the Council's 60 seats. If they drop below that number they can usually count on a few of the Independents to give them a 'de facto' majority. So with no luck with the Tories it was to the Labour Party and instant success in getting a meeting with the Council Labour leader Paul Harvey. We met at Costa Coffee in Festival Place, Basingstoke. Paul Harvey is a very pleasant man and seems to understand what is required. He knew the right things to say at the right times during the early part of the conversations. However, the key point to me was what the Labour Party's position was in respect to opposition on the Camrose redevelopment.

No answers were forthcoming and a few comments left me baffled to say the least. 'This Proposal is unstoppable!!' – 'It will soon be passed.'

I said, 'Surely not.' I went on to say, 'I would have thought this would have been food and drink for the Labour Party. The Party of the many against the few!!' Paul went off to discuss it with his football-liking Councillors and get back to me.

Friday arrived and my big moment had arrived. A meeting with our local Member of Parliament, Maria Miller MP. I expected the meeting to be held at the Conservative Club in Bounty Road. However, the venue given was the Orchard Building adjacent to the Basingstoke and Deane Council offices. I went prepared and had a copy of an article on the Camrose ground to give to the MP. I had been offered a 15-minute consultation. I replied saying this one could go on a bit longer. The Orchard is very much an open-plan building with a central atrium. I had arrived early and the constituents before me were called. This was a group of three and they entered the lift to go up to the top floor where they were met by Maria Miller. In a very quiet building I could hear the basis of the discussion; some sort of passport arrangements for someone or other.

Then it was my turn. I had already worked out my strategy. Give her the Camrose article first and then butter her up. Following that hopefully Maria would come round to my way of thinking! The first part was easy and she said thank you for the article before instantly passing it over to her seconder; a young man with a note book. First part achieved so on to the second part. I said, 'I remember when you first became the MP for Basingstoke! You came to my house in Kempshott. What impressed me was that I did actually have some query at the time. I told you what it was. You said you would deal with it and what happened afterwards really impressed me! An hour later my door went and there you were with the answer. I thought at the time you were just the sort of MP we need in Basingstoke!!'

That was about as good as it got. We quickly moved into the bones of the consultation and it soon became apparent we were on different wavelengths. I felt the Lord Camrose Covenant should have been preserved and honoured. Maria felt the Owner purchased the ground from the Camrose Estates and should be allowed to proceed as he saw fit. No consideration should be given to the Council purchasing the Basron 71% share of the Camrose ground. However I felt it was time to produce my ace card. 'What about the Sport England objections?' A discussion followed as I explained that Basingstoke would lose one of its two football grounds if the Camrose Development went forward. For several minutes we talked in cross purposes over the term FA. Maria felt FA was Hampshire FA; I was talking about the Football Association and the Football Foundation. Eventually it came down to me showing her that two minus one does not equal two.

Then the unbelievable happened; I could not believe my luck! Maria got a text to say the Basingstoke Ladies team had folded. She was clearly upset. It gave me the opportunity to say, 'Well with Mr Razzak around you never know what is going to happen!'

Her seconder quickly got onto his calculator and said, 'The good news about this is that it will free up an extra nine slots at Winklebury!!' I am still not sure whether he was joking or serious.

HAYLEY EACHUS

The meeting could have gone on for a long period afterwards rather than the 40 minutes it had taken. My parting remark was that it was certain that a lot more would be heard about this scandal. As I left the Orchard there were several black looks from the people waiting for their consultation with Maria Miller. In fairness to her, she did back up with a few follow-up letters showing communication she had with the Football Foundation and Sport England.

So my week in politics was over and I had quickly come to the conclusion there was something very wrong in Basingstoke on this whole issue. So many questions and very few answers:

1. The complete lack of representation offered by elected Councillors. This was the first time I had contacted a Councillor on any issue in all of the 47 years I had lived in Basingstoke.

2. The weeks ahead showed that Hayley Eachus was a Solicitor at Phillips the Solicitors. They were the Solicitors for Mr Razaak and his partner Malcolm McPhail at Basron the Development Company.

3. A big problem with politics in Basingstoke as I see it is the complete lack of competition to the Conservatives. In Kempshott where I live it is usually an automatic re-election of the three Councillors. They put the blue rosette on and they get elected. It is of course also true in Labour Wards like South Ham and Popley. Add in the mix of village Councillors who are invariably Conservative and a natural built-in majority is in place. This in many ways contributed to the Camrose Scandal. Few of the Councillors had any interest in football and did not take sufficient interest in what was about to be lost in the form of the Camrose ground.

4. Friendships on the fringes of the Council were built up and many of these friendships led back to Mr Rafi Razzak, the owner of Centerprise and Basron. These friendships appeared to exempt Basron from scrutiny during the Planning Process until very late in the day.

5. With a strong Conservative presence on the Council it would have taken a proactive Labour Party to have made their presence felt. The meeting I had with Paul Harvey and communication I had with the Labour Party during the December 2019 General Election showed that they seemed intimidated by the Tories.

The truly staggering fact in the Camrose Scandal is that the Council were willing to give up one of its two football arenas for no tangible benefit. Even basic moral judgements should have made them think the process through.

CHAPTER 2

BASINGSTOKE TOWN FC HALCYON DAYS

It would be true to say Basingstoke Town never seemed to be destined to be the most successful football team in England. Up until around 1970 they plied their trade in the Hampshire League. Then there was some ambition shown at the club. They entered the Southern League a decent step up from the Hampshire League. A large stand was built on the Winchester Road side of the ground.

Travelling past the ground at this time the impression given was of an ambitious club. A club ready to grow with the town and hopefully in the not too distant future move upwards towards the Football League. After I was married in 1973 we moved to Basingstoke and bought our first home at Brighton Hill. Being a football follower I made some trips to the Camrose and watched a decent level of football. Cliff Huxford, the former Southampton midfielder, ruled the roost in midfield and was an inspirational captain. Jenner Brown, a blond striker, scored goals for fun. The Camrose ground had a track around it. Some years prior there were plans to have dog racing and a speedway track. These activities were scuppered following objections to the Council. The basis of the objections were religious and the gambling aspects of dog racing. My early impressions of the ground were that the big stand on the Winchester Road side was phase one and more development would be following along in due course. The club seemed to hold their own for the most part without setting the world alight. A particularly good team in the mid-1980s saw the Southern League title captured amid much excitement.

When my two sons Stuart and Matthew came along I made a point in trying to encourage them to support their local side. We went to virtually every home match over a number of seasons and also to around half of the away fixtures. We watched the matches initially from the big stand which provided great views. However, a downside was the fact that there were no side panels at the end of the stand to shield from a bitterly cold wind. Then it was over to the Victor Meldrew Stand on the Mansfield Road side of the ground.

Most seasons continued to be modest punctuated with the odd memorable occasion. One such was an FA Cup 2nd Round match against Torquay United. An all ticket capacity crowd of around 4,000 packed in to see a good match won by Torquay by 3-2. Barry Blankley and Paul Clarkson were the scorers for 'Stoke and the occasion was enjoyed by all.

In the mid-1990s Ernie Howe, the former Portsmouth and QPR centre half, became manager and a new sense of professionalism soon became apparent. Good signings followed. Paul Coombs from Aldershot, a prolific striker. Steve Harris, a tall, blond, dominant centre half and soon Steve Richardson (Rico) from Reading.

Off the pitch a new sponsor had arrived when Rafi Razzak started putting money into the club with sponsorship from his company Centerprise. His arrival as a sponsor was of course welcome. However, it did mask inherent problems at the club. In season 1993-94 the club had been in financial difficulties. Clearly the approach from Mr Razzak was welcome; it could not have come along at a better time. Or so people thought!!

A major problem with Basingstoke Town which has persisted to the present day is the reluctance of the Social Club Committee to relax their control of the club affairs. In the 1980s there was a much reported spat to decide who was to gain control of the Camrose Clubhouse. Essentially two families, the Knights and the Parsons, gained control. There is no doubt when it comes to the operating of the Clubhouse and providing for the members of the Social Club they obviously do a decent job. To the fans who did not frequent the Social Club they became known as the 'boys at the bar' and they seemed to be in control of virtually all aspects of the club.

They were popular with the Social Club regulars and few disputed their right to be making the decisions. In the run up to the 1997-98 FA Cup run they had employed a good Marketing Manager in Chris Richardson and of course very able team management in Ernie Howe and his assistant Pete Peters. The overall impression of the non-Social Club members was of a club committee which seemed to struggle with its finances. However, they were giving it their best shot and that, after all, was all they could do. The addition of Centerprise and Mr Razzak would hopefully bring business expertise to the fore and would propel the club in the right direction. Very early on in his dealings with the club, Mr Razzak was quick to announce, 'Are we running a Social Club here or is it supposed to be a Football Club?'

Clearly he had identified a flaw in the structure at the club. The Social Club committee had skills in running a Social Club. A completely different set of skills were required in the running of a Football Club. At the very lowest levels of the pyramid such as the Hampshire League, small Social Clubs are operated and they provide the funds for the football section. These funds are small and usually in line with the income of the club. Dealing with a football club at a semi-professional level is a whole different ball game where contracts are awarded to decent quality players. The budgeting requires careful planning and caution exercised. In addition to the players budget there is the team management of course plus all the other running costs associated with Basingstoke Town. The Camrose ground was already showing signs of decay and in need of upgrading. The Supporters Club appeared to be the ones who were to carry this burden. It was of course virtually an impossible task.

Things looked promising for the club as a large support travelled to Adams Park at High Wycombe to play Wycombe Wanderers. A few years previous the clubs had met during a qualifying round in the FA Cup. The Wanderers at that time under Martin O'Neil despatched the 'Stoke easily with six unopposed goals. This time was going to be different as Basingstoke Town support packed out the entire away end. The continuous rain did not dampen the spirits and most felt shock result was attainable. Wycombe were the better team in the first half and deserved their 1-0 lead at the break. The Chairboys added a second through John Cosforth (his second of the game) from a free kick. However, 'Stoke fought back and were well on top for the remainder of the match. Paul Coombs pulled a goal back with a shot which went in off the underside of the crossbar. Then more pressure saw Paul Wilkinson see a speculative shot deceive the home keeper and a replay was secured. In the away end to share in the celebrations was Rafi Razzak. A more popular man in Basingstoke would not have been found.

The replay saw a record crowd at the Camrose ground and probably the greatest night in the clubs history. Fondly remembered by all who were present to see a Basingstoke win on penalties. The second round of the FA Cup saw the club drawn away to Northampton Town. Basingstoke had five or six coaches leave from the Camrose packed full of supporters. Another left from Basing. On the way up the A34 a number of cars with the blue and yellow colours displayed outside the windows passed the coaches. The match saw the entire away end packed with 'Stoke fans and indeed there was overspill down the sides of the ground. The match was not a classic. It revolved around Steve Richardson (Rico) and Steve Harris scrapping it out against a giant Cobblers striker called Gayle. Seal gave Northampton the lead in the first half. Alan Carey scored a second half equaliser and it was back to the Camrose for the replay. Another almost maximum crowd of just under 5,000 attended. The town was buzzing. Sky television were there with Andy Gray as commentator. If the Basingstoke folk were buzzing before the match they were shivering in sub-zero temperatures during it. 'Stoke gave as good as they got and the match became a stalemate with defences on top. Into extra time and much the same as before took place leading the teams to a scoreless draw and a penalty shootout. Northampton missed their first effort and Basingstoke led for a bit. However, by the time the last kick came round the Cobblers were in front. The winning kick went in, bringing an end to Basingstoke Town's best ever FA Cup run.

The following season another FA Cup run saw Bournemouth arrive in the First Round. 'Stoke played well and Ian Mancey scored a good goal to pull 'Stoke level at 1-1. However, a late own goal gave the Cherries the passage into the next round. Aldershot were in the same leagues and a record ground attendance of over 2,500 was set against the Shots for a Boxing Day fixture. For a few seasons the club fortunes were good and it seemed only a matter of time before the long overdue climb up the leagues would occur.

The nights in 1997 will live long in the memory of the Basingstoke Town supporters.

Basingstoke Town V Northampton Town Programme

MATCH REPORT

TUESDAY 15th NOVEMBER 1997

FA CUP 1st ROUND REPLAY

BASINGSTOKE TOWN v WYCOMBE WANDERERS

Having secured a draw at Adams Park the whole town of Basingstoke was buzzing. Could 'Stoke pull off a shock result? A ground record all ticket crowd of over 5,000 were there to watch. Basingstoke started well and created a few half chances cheered on by the crowd. However, it was the Chairboys who took the lead. A decent move saw Steve Brown in possession around the Basingstoke box. Brown passed to the dangerous Steve MacGavin who shot over Dean Beale (0-1).

The crowd were subdued for a few minutes but 'Stoke bravely clawed their way back into the match. Wycombe held the edge with better movement and passing but were unable to add to their lead. Basingstoke continued to gain territory and pulled level on 40 minutes. This came as a result of two bad mistakes by the Wanderers. Firstly a free kick was misplaced to Simon Line who sent a quick pass upfield. Keeper Taylor came out but he miskicked to PAUL COOMBS and the ball ricocheted to towards the visitors' goal. It became a race to see whether the defenders could get back in time as the ball trundled for an eternity towards the goal and eventually into the net (1-1).

The crowd erupted and 'Stoke survived a few anxious moment before the half-time whistle.

HALF TIME:

BASINGSTOKE TOWN 1

WYCOMBE WANDERERS 1

The second half saw Basingstoke counter the Chairboys more measured approach with very direct play which was beginning to have success. Steve MacGavin continued to be the main threat and he brought out a good save from Dean Beale midway through the half. MacGavin looked dangerous every time the ball went near him and it looked as though he had won the match on 75 minutes. Loose play in defence by 'Stoke gave the Chairboys dangerman a chance and he shot home from a difficult angle (1-2).

Basingstoke were not for giving up and threw caution to the wind. However, this gave the Wanderers chances on the break and a MacGavin cross saw Keith Scott head just over. Continuous probing from the 'Stoke brought reward on 85 minutes when the impressive Paul Wilkinson's cross was handled in the penalty box. Paul Coombs thumped home the penalty kick. (2-2).

FULL TIME:

BASINGSTOKE TOWN 2

WYCOMBE WANDERERS 2

Into extra time and it was a tense affair. However, the visitors rarely looked like scoring and although tiring, the part-timers of Basingstoke looked the more likely to score.

AFTER EXTRA TIME:

BASINGSTOKE TOWN 2

WYCOMBE WANDERERS 2

The penalty shootout seemed to take a time to start which added to the tension. Basingstoke went first:

Simon Line scored – Cornforth scored

Alan Carey scored – Steve MacGavin scored

Nigel Emsden scored – Brown scored

Paul Wilinson scored – Read scored

Paul Coombs scored

The crowd held their breath for a minute as Keith Scott stepped up. His shot was tipped over the crossbar by Dean Beale who wrote himself into Basingstoke Town folklore for years thereafter.

Basingstoke won 5-4 on penalties.

This sparked a pitch invasion from the excited home support. Wycombe Wanderers supporters will always be remembered for the amazing sportsmanship after the match when they stayed and gave Basingstoke Town generous applause for a memorable win.

Teams:

BASINGSTOKE TOWN:

Dean Beale, Danny Barker, Steve Richardson, Simon Line, Steve Harris, Andy Morley, Paul Wilkinson, Nigel Emsden, Ian Mancey, Paul Coombs, Bruce Tydeman, Sub: Alan Carey.

WYCOMBE WANDERERS:

Taylor, Cousins, Beeton, Ryan, Mohan, Forsyth, MacCarthy, Scott, Cornforth, MacGavin, Brown Subs: Simpson, Read, Kavanagh.

CHAPTER 3

THE STORIES OF TWO WEALTHY MEN

The Camrose Scandal is in essence a story of two wealthy men. The first was William Ewart Berry and the second Rafi Razzak. They came to Basingstoke in different eras and both feature heavily in what was to become probably the biggest scandal in non-league football.

William Ewart Berry: Lord Camrose

It would be true to say a sizable book could be written about Lord Camrose. His fame was renowned throughout the UK and indeed throughout the then-vast British Empire. A brief precis on a small part of his life.

William Ewart Berry was the second oldest of three brothers born to

John Mathias Berry and Mary Ann Berry (Rowe) in 1879 at Merthyr Tydfill in South Wales. John Berry was already reasonably well off and served as a Justice of the Peace in Merthyr.

The Camrose crest which features a dragon is displayed on the Basingstoke Town Football Club's kit. In his early years he displayed a keen interest in publications and wrote about events in World War 1. With his younger brother Gomer Berry they purchased the Sunday Times. From there they purchased a large number of newspapers around the country and eventually secured one of their prime targets, The Daily Telegraph. This was before the advent of television let alone the digital age and newspapers and radio were the main source of news. Hence what was written by the Berry publications carried weight. Having control of the media meant he could rub shoulders with the rich and famous. A comparison nowadays would be Rupert Murdoch although he would never have been as brash.

William Ewart Berry moved to Hackwood Park and in time honours were bestowed on him. He eventually received the title of Lord Camrose. During the war he gave over his Hackwood Park to the war effort and spent time living at the nearby Audley's Wood. The Audley's Wood Hotel still has a room named after him. Lord Camrose was close friends with Sir Winston Churchill and in recognition of his contribution to the nation he has a plaque on the walls of St. Paul's Cathedral.

In terms of politics he was a strong Conservative. However, it was tempered and like the whole Berry family they were generous benefactors to many good causes especially in Merthyr Tydfill where they have a statue in honour of the family.

Post-war times were hard with austerity. Food rationing was still in place and it continued until 1954. Recognising the hardships endured by the Basingstoke populace, he decided to provide the town with a piece of land on Winchester Road to be used for Sporting Purposes. This was received with gratitude by two Aldermen of the Borough.

Lord Camrose died of a heart attack aged 75 at Southampton in 1974.

By total coincidence in 2010 I helped my younger son Matt's company (BEMS Ltd.) out by carrying out a breakdown visit in Victoria near New Scotland Yard. When I entered the floor where the problem was I noticed a familiar crest in the Foyer. It was the crest of Lord Camrose and the offices were occupied by Camrose Estates. Once I had resolved the reported problem I was able to speak to the office manager. He was pleasant and told me much of Lord Camrose. The office had a photograph of Lord Camrose and I was told of aspects of his life.

I enquired about whether or not there were still some family members involved. He advised that there were seven. Only three still lived in England and three others are in the USA. I asked if any were interested in football. He advised that really no. One of them does occasionally get a guest seat at Woking Football Club. I asked about Basingstoke Town Football Club. He was fully aware of the club and talked about the ground being left by Lord Camrose. He was aware of Rafi Razzak and we had conversation on the current situation at the club. Knowing what has happened subsequently I wish I could have been more inquisitive.

RAFI RAZZAK

Rafi Razzak was born in Iraq during 1949 and is given as the only son of Arif Abd Ar-Razzaq.

Not much information is given on Rafi Razaak's early life in Iraq. However, a lot is available on his father Arif. Iraq politics always seems to be complicated with the two main factions, the Sunni and Shia groupings. However, in Rafi's early years things in Iraq were very turbulent to say the least. The father was a pilot and belonged to one of several factions striving for power. From 1958 to 1968 there were several coup attempts to wrest power. The first of these was the overthrow of the Hashemite Royal Dynasty in 1959. It was bloody, with members of the family executed; dragged through the streets; and then burned just to polish things off nicely. A Republic was up but soon the factions in charge could not agree on the way forward.

In a general sense the country was left-leaning, more socialist than conservative. The Baath Party were the favoured political direction but a major stumbling block was where the focus should be. One faction wanted a Pan Arab agreement with President Nassar of Egypt offering guidance. The other group wanted to concentrate on having an Iraqi identity. Initially this group held power but the Pan Arab believers overthrew them with the leaders being executed before things settled down again.

Both groups opposed the natural enemy Israel and the western influence from the USA.

1963 came along and time for another revolution. The original group who initially took power regained control following another coup. A lot of old scores were settled up and hundreds, possibly thousands, lost their lives.

One man who seemed to be active in the various coups was Arif Abd ar-Razzaq. He was rewarded with a position as Minister of Agriculture. He was then promoted to the Commander of the Air Forces. In 1965 he decided it was his turn to benefit from the next coup and he succeeded. The latest coup allowed him to became Prime Minister which was to last just 11 days. A counter-coup was launched by the previous group who had held power and Razzaq fled to Egypt.

ARIF ABD AR-RAZZAQ

The following year Arif Abd ar-Razzaq was back with yet another attempted coup. Bagdad was bombed and a substantial section of the military backed his attempt. However, the existing Government managed to muster up enough military strength including the Commandos and retained power. Razzaq was arrested with others and told to expect punishment. However, after a relatively short time he was released. Speculation suggests that President Nassar of Egypt influenced Iraq's decision in preparation for the war with Israel in 1967. The assault through the Sinai Desert was going to need the best Air Force fighters at their disposal. In the event they were not needed. The Israelis obliterated the entire Arab air power before they could take off and went on to inflict a humiliating defeat during the seven-day war in the Sinai when the Arabs were routed.

The Razzaq family are understood to have fled to Egypt from Iraq and then on to England. It is believed they left with considerable wealth. Once in England Rafi Razzak set about resuming a settled life away from the turmoil and dangers of Iraq. Initially the family moved to Dudley in the West Midlands. His career indicates he studied at the Imperial College in London, followed by a period working for IBM. In 1983 he set up Centerprise and the firm have been based in Basingstoke ever since.

It seems certain that Rafi Razzak probably had a good advantage in negotiating Defence Contracts with the extensive knowledge passed down to him from his father. The Middle East is rich pickings for companies dealing with defence. Centerprise claim that they are very long-term suppliers to the Ministry of Defence. His love of his father who died in Reading in 2006 is considerable. This is shown by a fighter jet being placed outside the Centerprise offices at Chineham. Rafi Razzak has been involved in many business enterprises.

However, it is two that have come under a lot of scrutiny in recent times. These are Basingstoke Town Football Club Ltd. and Basron Limited.

In January 2020 Rafi Razaak was able to report another very successful year for Centerprise. Crude figures from Companies House suggest a Turnover of £95 million and a Nett Profit of £10 million. Most of the Centerprise board are either family members or people employed at the company. The Non-Executive Directors include Andrew Finney, a former prominent Councillor. An interesting Non-Executive Director and above all reproach is Rear Admiral Phillip Willcocks. Willcocks had a long and distinguished career and no doubt would be an excellent person to listen to. He was involved in both the Falkland War and also the Gulf War.

Centerprise appear to be a well-run company and the data provided to Companies House looks professional. It is a great pity that this type of professionalism could not have been employed at Basingstoke Town.

CHAPTER 4

A YEAR AT THE CAMROSE

BACK ROW: *David Graham, Stuart Graham, Ross Palmer, Mark Richardson, James Brown, Matt Stansfield, Richard Garrett, David Ford*

FRONT ROW: *Carlton Byrne, Scott Minton, David Asker Stuart White, Paul Taylor, Dean Ross*

Between the years 1992 and 1993 I spent a season as a coach to the Under 15 team. This came about when I was asked to take the bulk of the players at Hawkfield Boys Club where I was a manager to the club. The Hawkfield team I was charged with was successful and invariably in the top two of their league and regular league cup finalists and winners.

Hawkfield Boys Club were a model boys club and run by two absolute gentlemen in George Blackall and John Maxwell.. The club was run in the most professional way. A quarterly meeting at the Cricket Club planned events such as fundraising and end-of-season prize-giving. Proper agendas were put in place and everything was planned to a tee. The club put sportsmanship high on its agenda. One pleasing aspect about the team I was charged with was the fact that no fewer than nine of the team who started as Under 10s were still there at Under 16s. The parents were supportive; the boys a pleasure to be coaching and encouraging.

The Hawkfield Committee consisted of the six age group team managers, George Blackall and John Maxwell. Also Ian Walkom who was involved with the Basingstoke Town Youth set-up. An invitation was made to us to take the bulk of the team to the Camrose for a season and as a regular supporter of Basingstoke Town it seemed a promising challenge. Dave Harvey who had been the manager of a successful Hawkfield Boys team advised me against it. Dave was engaged to run a Basingstoke Town youth team and led his charges to a cup final which was held at Villa Park. He stated that the club was a complete shambles and needed a lot of sorting out to be done. He had left Basingstoke Town and returned to be on the Hawkfield Boys Club committee. Several other people whose views I respected said much the same. Totally against my better judgement I decided to take the team to the Camrose for a season. It turned out to be not one of the better decisions I ever made.

Things started off reasonably well. Head coaches Steve Frangou, Gerry O'Grady and Arthur Hammond were very able and before long a team had been assembled after trials. I was not 100% in favour of the selections made and we certainly let a few decent players slip through our fingers. I signed up to get my coaching qualifications and this was achieved via sessions from Arthur Hammond. From the outset it was clear that basic organisation and communication were all but missing at the club. There was a feeling that things were not right behind the scenes. A few small examples: One would turn up at the ground and go to pick the kit up for a Sunday match. The door to the kit room under the main stand was usually locked. In the pre-mobile phone days this meant a trip over to the clubhouse. The key holder had gone home and then a panic until someone produced the key. The second was getting a complete kit. On one occasion there were only shirts and socks. The only shorts were not the same colour scheme but of course they had to do. On checking in the era of tie-up shorts, there were no tie-ups having been sent off to be cleaned, we were told. This meant a stop en route to the match to buy string. Relatively minor things of course but they happened too often.

Within weeks after the start of the season Steve Frangou decided that he could tolerate it no longer. A few of the other coaches including the excellent Gerry O'Grady felt the same and they also quit. Arthur Hammond stayed but split between the various teams he had an impossible task. Effectively we were back coaching the team as we had been at Hawkfield Boys Club. The team despite all the limitations did well. In general we were expected to do well and a top-three position was within our grasp. There were two what I would describe as 'super teams' in our league. One was Renegades who were effectively the Representative team for Basingstoke. They were supported by players from outside the area who were being coached by professional clubs like Southampton and Portsmouth. To the north of the county there was Mytchett Athletic who were run on the same basis as the Renegades. My feeling was that it was good they were in our league as these clubs had strong sides. Those standards were what we should have been aspiring to – and to reach the levels of these teams. The results overall were good and we remained in the top three throughout the season. One annoying feature was that some of the stronger sides were able to postpone matches due to the

Representative matches elsewhere.

Things stumbled on with the Basingstoke Town youth team. We reached Christmas and then the first training session at Down Grange in the new year. Before we entered the changing rooms the Council attendant who looked after the courts said we were not allowed to use the facility.

I said, 'Why?'

He replied, 'The club have not paid their Court fees!'

I had a quick word with the parents present and we agreed to pay the fee for that evening. We soon extended the hire to the end of the season. I was hoping that at some stage I could have some sort of reimbursement and explanation from the club. None was ever forthcoming. However, as I got a free match day pass at least part of it could be written off.

Further into January I was watching a Basingstoke first team match at the Camrose. A friend came to me and said, 'I hear you have been sacked!!'

I said, 'Well that is the first I have heard of it!'

My friend said, 'I overheard the boys at the bar say that your team has not produced enough good players!'

Running the team was challenging to say the least. If the team in a higher age group needed a player from our team they had first call. We were fortunate on a number of occasions to raise the bare 11 players and on a few occasions that included two goalkeepers (Scott Minton and James Brown) who fortunately were both good on the pitch. The team could still win the league into the last few weeks. However, we had Renegades and Mytchett Athletic to play twice each. First up was Mytchett away and a 1-4 loss despite a decent performance. The return match was at the War Memorial and a goal from Matt Stansfield secured us a 1-0 win. The eagerly awaited and much delayed matches against Renegades were to all but conclude the season. In general both matches were similar with very few chances. We had more chances than they had but they took one of their chances in both games to secure two 1-0 wins. Despite the losses I was pleased that the players showed a good sense of professionalism far above that of the club. They showed they had ability and could compete individually and collectively against the better players at their age group. In the last matches I felt my son Stuart had his best ever games at right back. Over the season he was the utility player who slotted in at the last minute to complete the jigsaw that was team selection. The last match of the season was a home fixture played at the Camrose ground against Farnham and a 5-2 win. We finished third.

During the summer I was asked to help out with coaching at one of the school fun weeks. First team player Peter Terry was to take the group and I was the helper on the courts at the rear of the ground. It turned out to be a difficult experience and not so much fun, as the weather during that particular week was scorching. The courts were sun traps and I probably lost a stone in weight. During the summer Alan Humphries had moved on as manager, replaced by Ernie Howe. Ernie via Ian Walkom reached out to try and get me to return but I politely declined.

I could not think of a more shambolic operation than Basingstoke Town Football Club. How they ever functioned was completely beyond me. However, coming over the horizon to become Main Sponsor was Mr Rafi Razzak!! As they say, the rest is history!! Over the years since I have spoken to a number of people about the way football clubs are run. A number say that there are other clubs that are run in a very haphazard way, especially at non-league level. This is usually due to them not having enough helpers.

The season was over and we re-formed Hawkfield and then had a very successful season in the top division of the North East Hants league. The team lost out on goal difference in the league to

Sandhurst. Sandhurst needed to win the last match by seven clear goals. Their opponents Liphook did not take the fixture seriously and lost 10-1. However, Hawkfield won the Cup after beating Manor Crusadors 3-2 at Alton Town's ground. I owe much to my two assistant managers Merv Brown and George White. Great memories.

One statistic is that Hawkfield won either a cup or a league (or both) in every season. At Basingstoke Town we won nothing. A few players moved on and played at non-league level. James Brown played as winger for Sandhurst and featured against the reformed Wimbledon's first ever match. David Asker played for Basingstoke Town until injury forced him out for a while. He was to move to Andover and helped the team to a league and cup double. He also played in the successful Andover team that beat Havant and Waterlooville 2-0 at the Dell to capture the Hampshire Senior Cup. Strikers Paul Couchman and Stuart White scored goals for fun. Carlton Byrne could and should have played at non-league level. Whitchurch United invited him in for a match and he scored three goals. He preferred to play with his friends at Sunday football.

Hawkfield Boys Club produced a number of very good players over the years. As well as David Asker there was Jason Bristow who went on to become a great servant to Basingstoke Town. He played in the same team as my younger son Matt. The Vine brothers started at Hawkfield. Ashley Vine played a number of games for Basingstoke Town before moving to Newbury Town. The two twins Ben and Ricky were good footballers but did not pursue football ambitions. However, Rowan Vine was at Hawkfield with his brothers when he was very young. He was to move on to Loddon and from there to Portsmouth. He helped QPR and Birmingham to promotions from the National League tier to the Premiership. Much travelled, he had a successful spell late in his career at Hartley Wintney FC.

A SEASON AT BASINGSTOKE TOWN FOOTBALL CLUB BEST FORGOTTEN

HAWKFIELD BOYS CLUB WITH SOME OF

THE SEASON'S TROPHIES – 1992

BACK ROW: *Ross Palmer, Stuart White, Carlton Byrne, Steve Cleveland, Stuart Graham, Paul Couchman*

FRONT ROW: *James Ralph, Ross Gardner, James Brown, David Asker, Lee Whiteford*

CHAPTER 5

BASINGSTOKE TOWN FOOTBALL AND
SOCIAL CLUB LTD

PRESENTATION OF THE MAN OF THE MATCH AWARD
TO ANDY MORLEY BY OUR COMPANY BASINGSTOKE
CONTROL SYSTEMS IN 1996

Rafi Razzak arrived at Basingstoke Town FC in 1994. His arrival coincided with an upturn in fortunes and a promotion was achieved within the Isthmian League during his first two seasons as a sponsor. Clearly the injection of sponsorship money from Centerprise had made a difference. Soon the Halcyon days came along and provided much hope for the long suffering Basingstoke Town fans. Improvements were expected in the form of some good additions to the squad to improve a pretty decent bunch of footballers. More importantly the considerable sum of money collected from the FA Cup exploits would surely be spent on improving the stadia. Sadly we were to be so wrong. The team continued with some good form and a good season in 2000-2001 saw them achieve a high league position of 3rd place. However a year later they had slumped to 18th place.

If that was not bad enough, worse was to follow with an announcement that the club were in danger of going bust. The obvious question was where on earth had all the money from the 1997-98 season onwards gone? No explanations were forthcoming. So what had gone wrong?

When I had my one-year stint as a coach at the club I occasionally took a seat in the stand. One thing I noticed was that at every home match the gate money was taken from the turnstiles to the entrance to the main stand. This practice of course had always been the case. One week I had to pick up some items for a Sunday match from the changing rooms. I met the then-manager Alan Humphries in his office. When I entered his office I noticed a huge bundle of money on his desk. No suggestion of course that Alan Humphries had done anything untoward, however I felt this was unprofessional and hopefully was not a common practice. In 1994 we still lived in a world where cash was king at the turnstiles. The money was collected and presumably distributed to the various parts of the club.

The 2001 Annual General Meeting of the Basingstoke Town Football and Social Club was always going to be a sombre affair for those attending. The club as such could cease to exist and the talk was it could become a limited company which would at least save it. In basic terms the figures looked respectable. The Turnover had gone up slightly to £529K with a Gross Profit Margin of £327K. However the Admin costs were £433K and with other small values a loss of

£115K was being presented. If that was not bad enough there was a Tax bill of £129K due, Bank overdraft of £64K, Trade Creditors owed £73K and other Creditors £40K.

DAVID KNIGHT – BASINGSTOKE TOWN FC LTD (LEFT)

A winding-up order was put on the club by HMRC. Club Chairman David Knight gave his reaction to the local press.

THE chairman of Basingstoke Town Football Club is assuring fans that the club is not in danger of being wound up.

The Inland Revenue this week applied to the High Court in a petition to wind up Basingstoke Town Football and Social Club Ltd. The matter is due to be heard next Wednesday in London.

But club chairman Dave Knight told The Basingstoke Extra: "Basingstoke Town will not be wound up.

"I must admit this petition came as a bit of a surprise to us. We do owe the Inland Revenue money – I'm not prepared to say how much – but our advisers and accountants are dealing with it.

"We were not really expecting this but when the matter comes before the court next week they will ask for an adjournment.

"We are on the point of restructuring the club at the moment. We are forming a new company called Basingstoke Town Ltd and that will take over all the assets and debts of Basingstoke Town Football and Social Club Ltd. That should be completed in a matter of weeks."

Mr Knight said that the club had taken the decision to form itself into a private company at its annual meeting last August and offer £1 million-worth of shares to local businesses at £5,000 a share.

Mr Knight added: "A number of people have indicated that they are willing to contribute through share ownership. But that won't actually take place until the new company comes into being."

The club is hoping initially to raise £100,000 through the share scheme this season.

Club president Rafi Razzak, owner of thriving computer firm Centerprise International, has pledged to make up any shortfall up to a six-figure sum.

An Inland Revenue spokes-man said: "The Inland Revenue can apply to the High Court if an individual or company owes them money and they haven't paid. In the case of an individual, we apply for a bankruptcy order. If it is a company, we apply for a winding-up order.

"The amount of money owed will come out in the court proceedings – if the proceedings go ahead.

"In many cases they find the money before the day of the court hearing and pay it off. In that case the hearing is postponed or the petition withdrawn. They don't have to appear and the amount they owed is not made public."

At the AGM, Secretary Ian Walkom set the agenda for the meeting in the usual efficient format. Chairman David Knight presented the detail of the figures. The auditors sounded the tone by talking about the club continuing as a 'going concern'. Basingstoke Town Football and Social Club Ltd. was finished. Or so we thought!! It needed a person or persons with a lot of money to invest in the club and re-float it by paying off the debts. Basingstoke Town Football and Social Club (BTFASC) were to go into hibernation.. Prior to the BTFASC there had been two previous Basingstoke Town identities. These were Basingstoke Town Football and Athletic Club and The Basingstoke Town Football Club.

This meeting was a far cry from the meeting held three years previously (1998) in the aftermath of the Halcyon Days of the FA Cup runs in 1998. Then a happy Chairman David Knight could present a profit over the season. The Turnover was £627K and after costs a Net Profit of £54K was announced. This compared to a Turnover of £442K and Net Loss of £17K the year prior.

At the 1997 AGM of the club Mr Razzak was welcomed to the meeting. He sounded an alert to the club. He stated that the club must focus on the football. He had introduced a system of reporting accounts on a more regular basis. There were perceived to be two major flaws in the Basingstoke Town Football Club operation. One was the absence of a Treasurer. Most clubs rely on the Treasurer who is able to ensure that bills are paid and money collected on a regular basis. Without a recognised Treasurer the club relied heavily on an Accountant to produce the balance sheets once a year based on information provided. Also the Auditor gave a verdict on the figures produced by the Accountant. The second major flaw was any form of a budget for the forthcoming season. Rafi Razzak's advice on this would have been strong as he was the owner of the sizable Centerprise Company.

The club appeared to have the basics for success. In Chris Richardson they had a good Marketing Manager. The potential for large crowds was there, as demonstrated during the period 1997 to 2000.

Without doubt the major downfall of the club was a focus on the Social Club as picked up by Mr Razzak. In 1994 soon after becoming involved in the club he was quoted as saying, 'Are we running a Social Club here or are we running a Football Club?' The answer to most was the former. The Camrose ground was in need of modernisation and money had to be found. It could have been done of course. The clubs which Basingstoke Town competed against in the 1990s seemed to have constantly improving grounds. Woking FC, Eastleigh and Farnborough FC managed to plan and develop their stadia. It was not always perfect for these clubs and like all football clubs they had challenging times. However, they finished up with good grounds. Many towns in the region have finished with good stadia helped by their local Council and the Football Foundation.

The match day offer at the Camrose was poor and the only positive was the supporters who generally remained extremely loyal in putting up with what was on offer. The club usually had one of the most expensive admissions in the League. The toilets could have been better. The Main Stand was a positive when it was first built around 1970 but the ground never seemed to have been developed with the spectator as the core thereafter. The Main Stand never had Perspex at the ends to shield the spectator from a very cold wind in the winter and it was the same to the end. The changing rooms below looked dated and the entire block was said to contain asbestos. At the other side of the ground the Victor Meldrew Stand is a long structure. It has been there for just about as long as I can remember. Again, this structure does not offer any protection from a raw wind in winter. I can recall several very cold nights watching football from this stand. The Northampton Town FA Cup match saw temperatures of around minus 10. However, with a huge crowd present we were all able to chatter our teeth in harmony and keep close together. Another match I recall was against Aylesbury United. The Ducks had a centre forward called Cliff Hercules who scored for fun. He duly obliged on that evening and helped Aylesbury to a fifth win over Basingstoke in a single season. A miserable night all round enduring the bitter cold as well as the team getting thumped.

The John Hacker Stand was, I understand, provided by the Supporters Club. This is on the same side as the Main Stand and offers good shielding from the winds. Possibly the only criticism is that it is sometimes difficult to see the near side of the pitch when the ball is down the right-hand side. Beyond the John Hacker Stand there has only been the occasional improvement usually to satisfy an FA Ground Grading issue. The feeling I have had for a very long time is that Basingstoke Town FC see the ground as a 'Cash Cow'. The amount of ground development over the past 30 years has not kept up with requirements. The onus appears to have been pushed on to the supporters to provide the improvements. It is sometimes worth noting that if you were to remove the Main Stand when looking at an aerial photo of the ground it would show very little indeed, testament to the complete lack of investment in the club.

With the demise of Basingstoke Town Football and Social Club there was much discussion of the part Directors David Knight and Brian Parsons played in respect to the club management. To the ordinary supporters like myself on the terrace both these Directors were reasonably popular at the time and a degree of sympathy was extended to them both. Clearly the amount of debt that had accumulated had proven to be the downfall of the Basingstoke Town Football and Social Club Ltd.

VICTOR MELDREW STAND OPPOSITE

CHAPTER 6

ANYONE FOR SHARES?

THE STORY OF EARLY BASINGSTOKE TOWN LTD

SERGIO TORRES – MAGICAL MIDFIELDER WITH SOUTH AMERICAN FLAIR

The apparent demise of the Basingstoke Town Football and Social Club led to the birth of a new Limited Company. However, before the new Limited Company could start it was necessary to attend to the situation regarding Creditors due money from the previous company. This was probably a requirement by the Football Association. Mr Razzak took charge of this and agreed Company Voluntary Agreements. This held off the immediate Creditors and in the press Razzak portrayed this as a success, something which of course did not go down well with the Creditors.

Local legal firm Phillips the Solicitors got involved and drafted up the rules of the Share Issue. A 35-page Incorporation document was produced. At first glance it looked like a bespoke normal terms and conditions one would probably expect when setting up a company. However, they were not. The conditions were strict and appeared to have been designed to give Rafi Razzak total control of the new Limited Company. Within the documentation from 2002 there appears to be little in the way of reference to the Lord Camrose Covenant. This was to become an issue of focus many years later.

In the contracting world, if those conditions were offered they would almost certainly have been rejected by the relevant companies Quantity Surveyors. Unfortunately Basingstoke Football and Social Club Ltd did not have a QS at their disposal. They would probably have hoped that their erstwhile Solicitors Phillips would have been even handed. Instead it appears they had effectively changed sides and were representing Razzak.

A Share Issue was finally put out. Each share was to be £5,000 in the new venture. A preferential share of £5,000 was issued and it was said this was to be for the benefit of the supporters. This benefit was to negate any one person having 100% of the shares. The supporters in theory would have a final say. The limit for the business was set at £1 million.

To the ordinary supporter on the terraces a Share Issue of such value was out of reach. £5,000 was a lot of money to pay out. This was true especially as no real prospectus was produced. No plans for the future. No vision. It was just a case of give £5K and Rafi Razzak will deliver the goods. The assumption was that Razzak would probably know other potential investors and between them they would produce an initiative to forward the town's football club. This assumption proved to be wrong.

In October 2001 David Knight, the former Chairman, joined initially as Director then as Secretary followed by the role of CEO. He was to remain steadfastly loyal to Rafi Razzak throughout the period 2001 until his departure in June 2020. Knight took care of all the day-to-day operations of Basingstoke Town Ltd.

The local media reported the formation as follows:

THE BIGGEST development in Basingstoke Town Football Club's 103-year history took place on Tuesday night when club members unanimously voted it become a Private Company Limited by Shares.

The ground-breaking move was orchestrated by club president Rafi Razzak (pictured) in tandem with the BTFC board and is the clearest indicator yet of the club's desire to reach the Nationwide Conference.

At the club's AGM on Tuesday night at The Camrose, Razzak and the board engineered changes to the constitution of Basingstoke Town – a change that will allow outside investors and businesses to back the club financially.

The ultimate aim is to raise £1 million – the authorised share capital – but more immediately a significant six-figure sum of more than £100,000 during the next three-and-a-half months so that by the end of November, Basingstoke Town will be able to start operating as a Limited company.

Mr Razzak, the multi-millionaire owner of Centerprise International, Town's main sponsor, exclusively told The Gazette: "We have outlined the complete change in the structure of the constitution tonight, a change which has been agreed and one that all of us believe is the way forward.

"By allowing private companies to create capital by buying shares, our aims and aspirations to move Basingstoke Town forward to the Conference and beyond are greatly increased.

"Under our old structure, this could not happen but that's no disrespect to the current board who have put in a tremendous amount of effort and commitment.

"But we need a full-time company, financially backed and with a proper management board, to run the club."

Entitled Basingstoke Town Limited – a name which has already been registered – the new private company will be known as BT.

It will take on all assets and liabilities of the Basingstoke Town Football and Social Club Limited, which began operating in 1988, wipe their existing debts before starting afresh as Basingstoke Town Limited.

In order to raise the £1 million, shares will be offered at £5,000 per single share, *the minimum investment required.*

The existing football club will be protected by virtue of a £5,000 "preference share", which ensures that the club, ground and land at The Camrose remain in operation for football use.

That leaves 199 shares available for outside purchase, and the club will now wait for the degree of response from the town's businesses.

Mr Razzak's initial personal contribution will be to pledge the minimum amount required to bring up the six-figure total needed after all interested businesses have invested.

He said: "We are hoping that as many local businesses as possible get behind us, to support their local team and local community.

"£5,000 is no amount at all for the companies in Basingstoke, a town which has such a low level of unemployment.

"Now that the motion has been passed we need to have their pledges and commitment by the end of November - something that will ensure football within the town is promoted and that the club's success will continue."

Basingstoke Town Limited will have a minimum of five directors, appointments the new shareholders will decide at a later date.

Shareholders will also decide how much of the money raised will be used for improving facilities and the team.

After the new proposals were delivered on Tuesday, Razzak and chairman Dave Knight took questions from those in attendance for 90 minutes before the unanimous vote was cast.

"The questions were very positive and addressed their issues and concerns, but there were no objections to any of the proposals," said Knight afterwards.

Mr Razzak revealed the plans for the change have been carefully thought through. He said: "It is something we have been considering for the past three years ever since our great FA Cup run against Wycombe and Northampton.

"That run showed the potential and raised the profile of the club in the eyes of the

establishment."

Now the motion has been passed, copies of the latest development will now be sent to the Ryman League and Football Association for their approval and suggestions to remedy any considerations that may have been overlooked.

The accounts of Basingstoke Town Football Club Ltd often appeared scant from the start with the owner Rafi Razzak offering to take full responsibility for them. My feeling is that this offer should be taken up by Companies House in order to clear up any misunderstandings. I am not an Accountant, having been an Engineer during my working life. However, I did run my own small business for 24 years and have the basic understandings of accounts and what is required. My youngest son Matt has a Limited Company and has a good understanding of the requirements needed by Limited Companies.

One personal opinion I have is that I am suspicious of rich Middle Eastern businessmen. This is not a prejudice against Middle Eastern people. I have many friends in this group and I greatly love their friendship and respect their religions and cultures. However, my suspicions about dealing with rich Middle Eastern businessmen dates back to the 1980s. I was the Commissioning and Service Manager at a Swiss company with an office in Staines. One day we received an enquiry for a project in Dubai from a company called Cementation. They were a sizable concern and it was their job to source labour and materials for an ongoing number of large projects in the Middle East. Within two minutes of receiving the enquiry I had a call from our head office in Switzerland. They asked if I had received an enquiry for a Middle East project in Dubai to which I replied 'yes'. The caller said, 'You must be careful!! If dealing with Middle Eastern projects you must not extend any form of credit. I complied with the request. I sent in our Proposal which included every cost imaginable. Flights, Transport, Hotel, Subsistence plus others. Then marked up by 300%.

Of course Cementation were soon back, queried the price but placed the order. We had many other projects and finished up with a very profitable department. The engineers got a good rate and a number were always willing to go to that part of the world. We insisted on payment up front for every project. In recent times of course Carillion Ltd. found out this harsh lesson and part of their demise were the losses sustained on Middle Eastern projects.

In 2002 Rafi Razzak purchased 11 shares and his family members and associates a further 4 shares between them. A Capital of £75,000 (15 x £5K) was made available. It must have been disappointing for Razzak that after a period of time the only shares purchased were those of himself and those of his family. By 2003 virtually all of the people involved with the previous company had left. It was evident that even by this stage the same problems of previous times were beginning to surface. The two basic fundamentals were very tight accounting and a good business plan. The club had neither.

The first Annual Accounts were presented in 2003 by Director David Hunt. Although a Director, David Hunt had not seemingly purchased any shares. The accounts were made up to 31st July 2003. A very short abbreviated set of accounts were issued and the Auditors gave their opinion that as far as they could see they were acceptable. However, there were obvious omissions, notably no Turnover figures and no Profit and Loss account. Brief as the accounts were one item stood out. Mr Razzak had shares to the value of £75K. However, it was noted further down the sheet that a value of £75K was under the heading of 'Creditors'. Hence it appeared that whereas Rafi Razzak was buying shares in what was effectively his own company he was also putting the value down as a loan. This value had a negative effect on the final figures which went from a profit of £111K down to a profit of £36K.

A major problem was historical debts owed by Basingstoke Town Football and Social Club Ltd. This was reflected in a meeting at the Council in October 2004.

SENIOR Basingstoke Town officials have held clear-the-air talks with Basingstoke and Deane Borough Council representatives to repair their damaged relationship.

Long-standing disagreements – Including one stretching back 30 years – and general bad blood have in recent weeks been the cause of renewed arguments between the parties.

The new Basingstoke Town Limited (BTL) board of directors believes there has been a lack of support from the council, who fired a broadside in return about all that has been done in the past for the club.

In a bid to halt the public slanging match, a meeting was arranged last week.

BTL owner and president Rafi Razzak, chairman David Hunt and company secretary Ian Walkom met with two council officers, including deputy chief executive Tony Curtis, in a 90-minute meeting that centred around five main discussion points:

The long-term future of Basingstoke Town FC

The change from the old Basingstoke Town Football Club and Social Club Limited (BTFCSCL) to the new BTL set-up

The terms of the club's Company Voluntary Agreement (CVA), the debts cleared since then and the impact that had on outstanding council invoices.

A £36,000 council grant for improvements to the Camrose

A better relationship based on mutual communication and trust.

Hunt said: "I would describe it as an outstanding meeting. We've been waiting some time for the chance to clear the air and, now that we have, we've agreed we're in a position to work together for the best interests of the club and town.

"We all wanted to resolve the situation. The council felt it was being seen in a bad light, when the truth is it has supported the club over a number of years and has invested money."

Hunt's consortium – In tandem with Razzak's cash – invested two years ago to save the club from administration and then paid the £45,000 CVA settlement the club agreed with its major creditors.

Hunt said he was especially pleased to have cleared the issue of old debts to the council.

"They've recognised outstanding service invoices, for work on the ground and pitch, were to do with the old company and was all prior to the new set-up.

"They've agreed that's not a liability for the current club and we thank them for their understanding over that matter.

"The council has also agreed to honour the grant of £36,000 it has held for us, when, in all honesty, it could have spent it somewhere else.

"We will now be having further meetings to discuss how that money will be funded to support the club.

"We will be trying to link that to the requirements selected by the Nationwide Conference league. Hopefully, by spending that money properly with council input, there will be opportunities to get further grants."

Despite building bridges with the council, Hunt said the club is still battling to find new sponsors and investors.

"We are running a tight ship because there's no way that this club is going in the position it was before. We really need to find one or two big sponsors. Without them we are struggling to go forward.

"It's a big challenge, and we're also trying to increase revenue through the social club. It's starting to build but it's not as good as it should be.

"Until we get more investment though, we cannot improve facilities, so we're in a catch 22 situation.

"The Friends of Basingstoke Town do a wonderful job, contributing towards the players' wages, but it would be great to be able to support Ernie more, especially if we keep doing as well as we are on the pitch and a play-off place is achievable.

"The biggest positive is the way the team is doing. There's a lot of commitment and enthusiasm.

"It's very disappointing to go out of the FA Cup, but their better displays in the

league have been reflected in the gate. On average, we're up about 80 people per game.

"Hopefully, we can keep that going and maybe put a run together in the FA Trophy or Carthium Cup and we'll attract some investment."

On the pitch the team under Ernie Howe had four seasons of fluctuating fortunes. On one occasion in 2000-2001 season they finished 3rd and two seasons later 5th. However, in between they had two positions of 18th. In both these seasons they had the heroics of their goalkeepers to save them from relegation and in particular Scott Tarr.

Two players who were making a good impression were young defender Jason Bristow and Sergio Torres. Torres was an Argentinian who had taken up a job at Boots Warehouse in Basingstoke. How lucky was it for Basingstoke that he started playing for them. He was probably one of the best players ever to wear the club colours. Most weeks he ruled the roost in midfield with some amazing skills. He was worth the admission money just to watch him play.

In 2004 there was an uplift in the club's fortunes off the pitch. A new Board was small but starting to make an impact. The group of four Directors were Ken Taylor, Linda and Steve Murfitt plus Sarah Parsons. All of a sudden the Share Issues got a new lease of life. The Murfitts appeared to have been successful in persuading several friends to invest and the shares purchased added £150K to the Company. The second set of accounts were produced in 2005 and signed off by David Hunt and Sarah Parsons. Like the first set they were scant in detail. No Turnover figures produced and little information on the Profit and Loss Account. However, what was noticeable was that another loan to the value of £45K had been added to the Creditors' account. It did not specify where this loan had come from. The combined total of the two loans now stood at £120K. The company seemed to be struggling in a sea of debt; some of it seemingly inflicted by the owner.

The question that has come up several times over the years in this scandal is this. **'Is it legal for a Shareholder to convert Shares into Loans?'** I would have thought not. However, apparently it is legal but certain conditions must be met. Most financial commentators seem to frown upon the practice. They mention the tax implications can be complicated.

VIEW FROM JOHN HACKER STAND

CHAPTER 7

BASRON DEVELOPMENT LIMITED ARRIVE

MALCOLM MCPHAIL (CENTRE) WITH SARAH PARSONS

Malcolm McPhail hails from Paisley near Glasgow in Scotland. He is highly educated and gained a Bachelor of Science at the University of Paisley. He spent most of his employment life as a Surveyor before setting up his own company as a Developer. For many years he has run a small family business in Basingstoke. He describes his company below:

As Founder and Managing Director of Lamron Estates for close to 30 years, I have forged a formidable reputation within our sector through my years of experience and our outstanding record of success. From our inception in 1991, Lamron Estates has punched above its weight to become one of the most highly regarded commercial development companies outside the M25.

He is relatively well known in the Basingstoke Council offices. The staff members felt he matched the description he put on his firm's website. 'A small developer who punched above its weight. Determined to get a good deal for his clients'. The Company accounts were well presented and always on time. Like most small businesses they tick along generally having decent years of trading. Two noticeable features were firstly the number of companies set up by Malcolm McPhail. A staggering 85!! Most seem to be some sort of ongoing leasing to clients once projects are completed. The second is the 'RON' added to the end of a few of his companies, i.e. Basron, Lamron, Fishron etc. By contrast Rafi Razzak has only been involved in 19, some of which are no longer active. So between Razzak and McPhail they have been involved in a staggering 104 companies!!

A deal was struck between McPhail and Mr Razzak. Centerprise would put up capital as required when the time came to purchase a new ground. The risk was to be equally split between Rafi Razzak and Malcolm McPhail. However, as in the case of Basingstoke Town Ltd. the conditions were considerable with Malcolm McPhail seemingly exposed disproportionately to any risks involved. These conditions were once again drafted up by Phillips the Solicitors. With Centerprise being the Lender then effectively it was always going to be Rafi Razzak calling all the shots.

Prior to 2006 Razzak was granted some loans by using on occasions the Camrose ground as security. There were six occasions when the ground leasehold was offered as a security against loans.

1) The first was Mr Tariq Manser Butt and a Legal Charge was made. This was delivered in 2002 and paid off in 2005. No value was given.

2) Then a Debenture with National Westminster Back was made. This was delivered in 2002 and paid off in 2005. No value was given.

However, the remaining four are still outstanding:

3) Centerprise has a Legal Charge made in March 2004. The value given was £25,000.

4) Mr Razzak made a Legal Charge in March 2004.

5) HSBC Bank made a Debenture in May 2004. No value was given.

6) Mr Razzak made a Legal Charge in May 2005. The value given was £25,000.

NOTE: An extra Mortgage (Debenture) is still recorded as being owed by Basingstoke Town Football and Sports Ltd. The value is unknown.

Of course there may be an explanation as to why these loans were taken out. It does seem bizarre that an individual who has such wealth needs to raise capital for what is effectively his own limited company. Even more bizarre is that it appears the loans were entered down in the Creditors columns.

The consequences of these transactions were profound.

- In terms of receiving the loan the money does not appear to have been spent on very much. The Accounts were scant and give no indication of where the money went. From the people on the Camrose terraces no real improvements were noticed on the stadia. The team generally held its own but no high value signings were apparent.

- In terms of the loan values going on to the Creditors' ledger meant that the club was perpetually in debt. Even worse, that debt was increasing with each passing season.

- It appeared that Razzak who effectively owned the club was not putting his own money into the Limited Company to allow investment. The shares he purchased were being converted into loans.

- As indicated previously there has been discussion on whether it is permissible legally to convert shares into loans. The difficulty with the Basingstoke Town Ltd. model is that there was effectively no Board of Directors who could challenge. People who joined as Directors generally were individuals who joined to benefit the running of the football club. However, they had little or no influence on steering Rafi Razzak in any direction. He was the man in charge and he did what he liked.

In the first four years of the Rafi Razzak regime he had taken out loans using the Camrose ground as security. This gave him the opportunity to turn the spotlight on the Leasehold and enable discussions with the owner of the Freehold – Camrose Estates. Camrose Estates owned the ground and a Covenant was in place until 2053 more than 30 years hence. Of course in terms of a football ground a tenure of 30 years for any club is a tremendous asset. Basingstoke Town made a virtue of this with the notes they gave to their opponents for away matches. Viscount Camrose always got a mention in the notes and into the programmes.

Over the seasons I had become a lot more selective in the football that I watched. Generally up to around 2007 Basingstoke Town would be my first port of call. However, that had changed and increasingly I was watching football elsewhere. I found I got a better match day experience at other grounds. In the past I had watched Andover, with former Hawkfield Boys Club player David Asker, win a Wessex League and Cup double under Mr. Cunningham Brown. Over many years I watched some league matches with one of my clients at Yeovil Town. Yeovil always provided a top quality match. Six times a season we would go to the beer tent and then to our seats at the halfway line to watch the Glovers. In return he would take me along as his assistant as a guest to Bristol City at Ashton Gate. There we had a seat in the Hospitality boxes. I had followed Winchester City with the formidable strike force of Ian Mancey and Andy

Forbes, both ex-Basingstoke. Mancey of course featured in the 1997 FA Cup run and a firm favourite with Paul Coombs at the Camrose ground. Andy Forbes went to Basingstoke as a youth player with aspirations as a striker. He was told that he was a natural full back. Andy went on to Andover then Winchester City. He scored an enormous amount of goals and went on to win the National Non-League golden boot for goals scored in a season. We went to Birmingham City to see the FA Vase Final when Wembley was being modernised to see the Citizens win 2-0

Farnborough was an occasional trip, as were Whitchurch and Alton. However, an increasing destination was Hartley Wintney. I found the match day there was second to none helped by a very friendly bunch of people.

MATCH ACTION AT THE CAMROSE GROUND

CHAPTER 8

SOCIAL MEDIA AND DISCONTENT

STOKIE THE DRAGON:

A GREAT INITIATIVE – USUALLY RICHARD MIDGELY

During 2006 there was an upsurge in interest in Basingstoke Town. Ernie Howe had moved on and was replaced by Francis Vine. The change did not seem to bring instant success to the team. However, coinciding with the arrival of the new manager the club had a new Chairman for the Supporter's Club. Ian Davies was elected to what many would have described as 'Mission Impossible'. However, he was able to put his talents to good use. He was skilled on Social Media and unafraid to speak his opinion. He was helped in no small way by Cliff Barrett, a local taxi driver. Between them they were able to communicate effectively to the club's fan base. This resonated with a lot of the younger age groups and before long the crowds at the matches started to increase.

The new influx of younger supporters brought good atmosphere to the matches despite the team struggling most of the time. Basingstoke won a few of the Qualifying Rounds in the FA Cup and reached the 4th Qualifying Round. They were presented with a difficult-looking away match at Worcester City. The interest was such that they were able to fill a supporters' coach and many like myself travelled up to the Midlands by car.

The match was not a classic in an old but well kept-up St George's Lane ground but it was exciting. City went in at half time a goal up. The second half saw Christian Levis take over with a sparkling display of skills. Levis was a friend of Sergio Torres and fellow Argentinian. He was a natural centre forward who was a constant threat but somehow Francis Vine saw him as a winger. However, from the wing he inspired Basingstoke to better things and an own goal brought the sides level and a replay at the Camrose ground.

A good crowd turned up for the replay. A better quality match than the first saw the sides level at 1-1 after 90 minutes. With no further score the match went to penalties. An exciting sudden death shootout saw 'Stoke scrape through 7-6. A feature was the friendliness of the Worcester City fans who were sporting and wishing Basingstoke Town success in the next round. The draw was not ideal in the sense it was an away match. However, it was against a Football League side at Chesterfield.

Ian Davies and his helpers organised the coaches. Two double-deckers plus a single-decker were heading north to the town with the Crooked Spire to cheer the team on to the rafters. Chesterfield were the better team but could not get the breakthrough goal. Basingstoke with fewer chances always looked threatening. Approaching half time a chance for 'Stoke saw Matt Warner score and send the travelling 435 supporters wild with delight. A tense second half followed as the Spireites piled on the pressure. However, with nails chewed down to the bone and watching through the fingers Basingstoke Town held on. The return trip on the coaches saw much singing from a happy bunch of supporters.

The second round draw brought a bit of excitement to North Hampshire. Aldershot were drawn at home to Basingstoke Town. Again Basingstoke were the underdogs and again they took good support to the Shots. They cheered the team on in a game of few chances. Approaching half time Joe Bruce put 'Stoke ahead following a corner. The Shots piled on the pressure in the second half and equalised to force a 1-1 draw and a replay.

The replay saw the crowd restricted to around 3,000 due to safety considerations. If the Camrose ground had been upgraded as it should have been then they could have once again had a larger crowd. 'Stoke started the better and a really good move down the left saw Neville Roach score an excellent goal. However, that was as good as it got for Basingstoke and the Shots were ahead by half time. They added another in the second half for a 3-1 win. If the Worcester City fans showed good sportsmanship, the behaviour of some of the Aldershot supporters left a lot to be desired.

With the FA Cup run over the club focussed its efforts in staving off relegation. The support stayed with the club and they maintained good crowds until the end of the season. A last match draw at Salisbury ensured that the team survived which capped a successful season of sorts. The question was, could they now move forward? Mr Razzak had been in position for five long weary years. The ground was decaying and there was a complete lack of any sensible plan for the future.

The supporters picked up on this and it showed very much on the Forums. Two camps quickly formed. There were the 'Loyalists' who were very defensive of the Social Club group and felt the club was best served by staying the course and things would come right. On the other side were the 'Reformers' like myself who could not see any future whatsoever with Rafi Razzak in charge and changes were also needed to the personnel running the club. Things started to get personal on the Forum and the club in their wisdom shut it down. A new one with more censorship re-started but this one too was soon closed down. A bone of contention was once again the Accounts situation. It was reported that Accounts were not being paid, including Tax bills. Also a number of Invoices were found stuffed into drawers, long overdue and waiting to be paid. It was a shambles.

A Fans Forum was called and Rafi Razzak was going to be there. In the meantime there was an appeal for more Directors. The two people who had done so much in helping with the Social Media, Ian Davies and Cliff Barrett, applied but were turned down. A number of other very capable people had also applied and they were accepted. Kevin O'Byrne who had excellent Social Media skills; Jim Gould who was good for planning small scale building projects and Margaret Dimbleby who was good at organising were all very able and capable people. A new Accountant Director was to start in order to try and sort out the Accounting mess. The meeting saw the new board presented. I went along to the meeting with my eldest son Stuart being critical of the club's affairs. We challenged Rafi Razzak at every opportunity with direct questions. However, we were the only ones in the entire packed club house. In the end I asked Mr Razzak when he intended to depart. He replied that he would be at the club for no more than three years. He added at that point he would be handing over the 'Golden Share' to the supporters of the club. At the time we did not know what the 'Golden Share' was. We were to learn that it was a Preferential Share. This share was to be in position to protect the Limited Company ever being 100% owned by any one person.

That of course was the last thing anyone would wish to happen!!

At the end of the meeting I felt the club had lost its last chance of going forward. I felt Ian Davies and Cliff Barrett would have been assets. Ian could be controversial with his comments. However, he had a feel for what was required and could have come up with good suggestions which could have been acted upon. Cliff Barrett could offer so much with his knowledge of building trades and had good practical skills. Both could communicate with the supporters. I had joined the Supporters Club while these two gentlemen were there and the Club reached a high membership. However, like most of the new intake of Directors they would have been Working Directors and not Shareholder Directors. They would never have had a chance of getting their input accepted by Rafi Razzak. He already had his eyes fixed on different goals from those put up at the Camrose.

After the Forum I decided not to renew my Supporters Club membership like many others. John Turner took over from Ian Davies and a more pleasant man you could not wish to meet. I apologised to him for not renewing my membership and said it was absolutely nothing to do with him becoming the Chairman. He fully understood and we had several good chats, often amusing, at the subsequent matches.

CHAPTER 9

SEARCH FOR A NEW HOME

DOWN GRANGE – BASINGSTOKE RUGBY CLUB

Rafi Razzak having set up Basron now started his quest to find a new home for Basingstoke Town FC. This as far as we are aware was never discussed with his Board. It was certainly not discussed with the supporters who virtually to a man or woman wanted to stay at the Camrose ground. The best option was to modernise the ground. However, his intentions were already made as indicated in the Article below.

Article from the Southampton Echo in 2005:

A MILESTONE deal has seen a leading Basingstoke businessman deliver a major boost to a town club's bid to create a sports facility at the heart of the local community.

Centerprise International chairman Rafi Razzak has this week pledged to invest £20,000 in support of Basingstoke Rugby Football Club's Stand Up 4 'Stoke appeal.

In the first-ever venture between Centerprise and 'Stoke, Mr Razzak's firm will become the main sponsor of the club's new stand at Basingstoke RFC's home in a naming agreement that will last for the next decade.

The deal is a big boost for the Down Grange-based club's appeal and it marks another significant local sporting commitment by Mr Razzak, whose firm has long been the main sponsor at Basingstoke Town Football Club.

Mr Razzak, the entrepreneurial founder of the Chineham-based IT firm, completed negotiations over the landmark rugby club deal on Monday afternoon at Down Grange with 'Stoke chairman Dr Steve Tristram.

Mr Razzak said he had been sufficiently moved to invest in the rugby club because he has "been so impressed by the appeal and what it is achieving".

He added: "The scale of this appeal, the people and commitment involved to make it work, and what it is doing to improve sports activities and facilities in the town, is very pleasing to see.

"I told Steve that if Centerprise could help in any way, we will. Now is the right time to honour that promise."

Launched last autumn, the appeal to raise £250,000 - to carry out a host of improvements to the rugby club's facilities and redevelop the club's Down Grange site - has gained great momentum over the past 12 months.

In August, following a long-running process, Basingstoke and Deane Borough Council – which has given vital cash backing and support to the Stand Up '4 Stoke appeal - finally gave the green light for the new 190-seat stand that is at the heart of the redevelopment programme.

Another significant boost came a few weeks later when the Inland Revenue awarded

'Stoke amateur sports club status, affording them 28 per cent gift aid, instead of being hit by 17.5 per cent VAT, on individual donations to the appeal.

After winning the backing of Mr Razzak, who is one of Basingstoke's leading entrepreneurs, Dr Tristram said this is the appeal's third "really significant breakthrough of recent months".

He added: "Rafi's, and Centerprise's, support is something we are extremely grateful for. The £20,000 is a substantial sum - one that will really kick-start the next stage of the stand's construction, because the finances were not in place to proceed before."

Funds for the new stand are still being raised by the club through the sale of sponsored seats and bricks in a special commemorative wall. Groundwork at the site has begun and the Centerprise deal means that the club should soon be in a position to actually order the stand. It is likely to be in place early next year.

Standing on the spot of the soon-to-be christened "Centerprise International Stand", Mr Razzak said he was pleased to further Centerprise's reputation within Basingstoke as a business that puts something back into the local community.

Mr Razzak said Centerprise's involvement with the rugby club will not affect his commitment to Basingstoke Town FC, where he is the owner and president of Basingstoke Town Limited.

He said: "I know I will be asked why I didn't put the £20,000 into the football club to try and help Ernie Howe's team and the club - but there are other sports clubs and projects in Basingstoke that deserve support.

"This year at the football club, I have brought in investors who have bought shares in excess of £50,000, there is my ongoing sponsorship of £25,000 and I have also bought out the man who helped David Hunt (Town chairman) and myself save the club from administration three years ago, for £80,000 – so my commitment to Basingstoke Town is still very strong."

Anticipating a growing relationship with both clubs, Mr Razzak said: "Part of my involvement is to see how, one day, we could perhaps combine all the sports facilities in Basingstoke in one area - and not just the football or rugby clubs sharing a stadium.

"Creating one large sports complex is a project that has been under discussion for some time. Of course, there are many complications, but that is something for the future."

First published: Thursday, November 3. 2005

Basingstoke Town were soon to change their manager. Francis Vines who I thought did not do too bad was replaced by Frank Gray. Gray was a Scottish International who had played at Leeds United with his brother Eddie. For the most part the Basingstoke team seemed to set itself up to bore the pants off the opposition. Obviously it also bored the pants off the supporters. The best sound was usually the final whistle signalling that you could now go home. Basingstoke were well organised and although always in the lower portion of the league stayed clear of relegation. They did win the Hampshire Cup with a 1-0 win over Farnborough at Bournemouth.

However, things did change for the better during the season 2011-12. 'Stoke signed an excellent striker in Delano Sam-Yorke who could score for fun. In addition to Delano Sam-Yorke they added some very decent players to support him. They went on a 14-match unbeaten run and were scoring goals aplenty. At the other end of the pitch goalkeeper Ashley Bayes was solid and popular with the supporters. In the FA Cup they had a good run and wins over Frome Town, Hartley Wintney and Staines Town saw them through to the 1st Round proper. They were rewarded with a good draw away to Brentford. The team had a little bit of a blow before the kick off with the news that Delano Sam-Yorke was not fully fit. However, he did play and looked a threat although far from 100% fit. In the first half there were few opportunities but it was the Bees who found the net. However, for the most part Basingstoke were the better team and probably felt unlucky to lose by the one solitary goal.

The season continued with the team in fine form which earned them a playoff place. A good crowd turned up for the semi-final against Dartford. The first match at the Camrose saw a narrow 1-0 loss. The second leg was also close but the Darts won 2-1 to progress to the Final on a 3-1 aggregate.

Off the pitch Mr Razzak's charm offensive to the Rugby Club's chief Steve Tristram seemed to be working. He was now firm friends with Andrew Finney, a prominent Councillor in Basingstoke. Soon the master plan unfolded. Basingstoke was to have a Sports Hub. All the sports in one place at Down Grange. The supporters at Basingstoke Town FC were not impressed. They still felt an upgrade at the Camrose was easily the best option. It never really looked like a realistic option from the start. It was probably inevitable that the Kempshott residents would object. Clearly the access along Pack Lane made it unsuitable for sizable football crowds. A modified plan was put forward to enable access off the A30 near Kempshott roundabout. Initially the plan seemed to be for the Rugby and Football Clubs to share the venue. This was also unrealistic with both the Rugby and Football Clubs having many teams. However, Mr Razaak was not for giving up and negotiations continued for four years before he hoisted up the white flag.

Article from the Basingstoke Gazette in 2009:

BASINGSTOKE Town FC chairman Rafi Razzak is optimistic that an eleventh-hour meeting has rescued and revived the prospect of building a new stadium complex at Down Grange.

*In November, The **Gazette** exclusively revealed how Town chairman Razzak wanted to move the club to Down Grange as part of an ambitious scheme to build a multi-million-pound community sports stadium complex – one that might feature a hotel and a fitness centre.*

It was hoped that the stadium might be shared by Basingstoke Rugby Football Club, with the complex also becoming home to the local hockey club, Basingstoke and Mid Hants Athletic Club and other sporting organisations.

The complex would have delivered the athletic club's long-awaited eight-lane track. Work to turn this dream into a reality has been going on ever since, but the plans were dealt a devastating blow earlier on Tuesday, when the borough council said a thorough study showed that Down Grange cannot fulfil the needs of all parties. Basingstoke and Deane officers investigated whether there was sufficient space to accommodate the needs of the rugby, hockey and athletics clubs, which are already based at Down Grange, and provide stadium facilities to meet the aspirations of Basingstoke Town.

They looked into a number of layout options but came to the conclusion that the site cannot fulfil the needs of all parties, including local residents.

*However, The **Gazette** can exclusively reveal that Razzak met with Steve Tristram, his opposite number at Basingstoke RFC, yesterday afternoon – and the soccer chairman came out of the summit with renewed hope that the ambitious scheme can still go ahead. "I am now optimistic that the plans can be resurrected," he said. "We reached a compromise and came up with a proposal to adapt the council's plans, so the ball is back in the council's court.*

"As I have said from the outset, the proposed development is something that would be to the benefit of the whole of Basingstoke and its sporting community, and not just the football club." Tristram added his support to the redraft, saying: "We believe we have reached a possible compromise with a number of shared facilities, which would allow the plans to be reconsidered."

Razzak and Tristram hope to meet council bosses to discuss the revised plans in the near future, and borough leader Councillor Andrew Finney said he would be happy to see what they have come up with. "If they have come to a compromise, and providing it works planning-wise, I would be delighted," he said. "We were disappointed not to be able to find a way of accommodating everyone and I hope an agreement can still be reached."

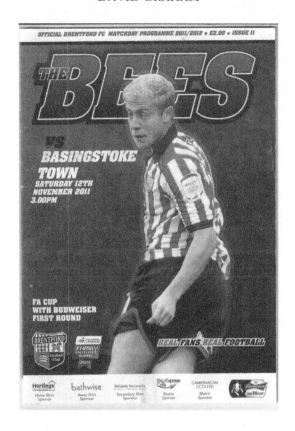

CHAPTER 10

THE REVOLVING DOOR OF CHAOS

CAMROSE SOCIAL CLUB

The failure of the Down Grange Hub project was always on the cards. However, it drew attention to the situation with the Camrose ground. The obvious question was, how was the project ever going to be funded? We suspected that the Camrose would be developed probably by the Council. They were of course believed to be the holders of the Lord Camrose Covenant.

A feature of Basingstoke Town FC Ltd. was the constant turnover of Directors and helpers. Following the Accounting disasters in 2007,

Rafi Razaak brought in an Accountant to sort things out. Vijaya Nayer had an unenviable task. A previous set of Accounts in 2006 were well presented by Ken Taylor and Linda Murfitt. They showed Turnover of £422K down slightly from the previous year. However, worryingly, the Creditors' debt was recorded at £297K.

The next two sets of Accounts were also well presented by Mr Nayer. The first was presented in 2008 and amazingly four Directors had resigned and four joined in the 12 months prior. Only Sarah Parsons remained in position. It was a fast-spinning revolving door.

The figures showed a Turnover of £473K and money owed to Creditors, a huge £385K.

Without doubt the loss of so many talented Directors who could have done much for the club in so many ways was a real blow. Mr and Mrs Murfitt threw in the towel and soon Mr Nayar was making for the exit door. The lack of any form of stability was apparent. Mr Razzak wanted a new ground. The supporters were quite happy at the Camrose if it could be upgraded.

In 2009 Rafi Razzak got a shock and he was furious. Firstly he stated that the club's debts had all but been wiped out. All very positive.

BASINGSTOKE Town chairman Rafi Razzak has revealed that the club is well on the way to wiping out its debts.

This time last year, the club owed more than £140,000 to various creditors and was in crisis, sparking the wage cuts that ultimately led to the departure of manager Francis Vines.

Since then, the board of directors have managed to reduce the debt to less than £45,000 and are paying off £5,000 every month, meaning that the club will be debt free in just nine months.

Razzak says that this has been possible because the club is working to a tighter budget and has new revenue through charging for the car park and by offering more services at the clubhouse.

The FA Cup run raised £12,000 and another £9,000 was raised through the club's progress in the FA Trophy. Additional money was received in the summer, when Wycombe sold Sergio Torres to Peterborough, activating a sell-on clause agreed when Town sold him in 2005.

However, even with this additional revenue, the club remains reliant on Razzak.

"I pay the shortfall each month but there have been months when I haven't had to put my hand in my pocket," the chairman said. "It's certainly better than last season, because I was putting my hand in my pocket every month."

Razzak could have paid the debt off but thinks that the club will benefit from paying it off on a monthly basis.

"The key for us is to make sure the club is run as a business rather than building up more debt," he said. "If I had just paid it off in one go, we might have ended up with further problems.

"It's about teaching people how to handle money and even when compared to the interest we have paid, that has value for me because I want the club to be independent of me one day."

The Town chairman is excited about the prospect of the club being debt free and even indicated that it could mean a loosening of the purse strings, player budget wise, next season.

"I am looking forward to the club being debt free because we will have up to £5,000 extra in the kitty every month," Razzak said. "We could potentially raise the budget for next season, if we need to. However, with the credit crunch, it may be that our current budget appears more reasonable."

However, while the club is well on the way to paying off outside bodies, Razzak himself is still owed a large amount of money. However, he insists that he is not looking for that back at the moment and says that the money he is putting into the club on a monthly is being converted into shares rather than adding to the debt.

"I am not going to ask for the money back," he said. "I hope I will be repaid as part of the long-term vision of the club but I will certainly not be looking to recoup

money once we have paid off these debts."

Then in the same year, a shock from the Tax man.

BASINGSTOKE Town FC has been issued with a winding-up petition – but chairman Rafi Razzak is assuring supporters and everyone involved with the club that there is nothing to worry about.

Her Majesty's Revenue and Customs (HMRC) has applied for the petition against Basingstoke Town Limited, with a hearing due to take place in the High Court next Wednesday.

However, Razzak claims the matter will never come before a judge and is confident that the future of the club is secure.

"I think to say that I can assure the supporters that the club will not be wound up is an understatement," he said. "The whole thing is one big farce."

Razzak said that the problem stems from £140,000 the club owed HMRC when he took over as chairman two years ago.

The board came to a deal with the taxman, agreeing to pay the debt off at a rate of £5,000 a month. The club have been doing this ever since and the amount outstanding is now down to £12,000.

Everything would have been paid off by February and Razzak claims that the club even received a letter about a month ago, thanking them for their efforts to erase the debt.

However, the Town chairman and benefactor admits that the club have occasionally been late making payments, and he said it is this that has sparked the winding-up order, with HMRC demanding that the balance is paid immediately.

"They say they are doing this because we have sometimes been a few days late paying the monthly instalment but that is not a good enough reason for the petition," he said. "It has never been a long time, just a few days.

"The club income fluctuates depending whether we have a match and when the players are paid. The board are doing the best they can to improve the club but we are staffed by volunteers and that will not change."

Razzak said the club has three options. They could fight the petition in court, which he feels would be successful, continue with the current arrangement – which he said HMRC has agreed to – or pay the balance off.

The board have decided to draw a line under the issue by paying the remainder of the debt off, though Razzak declined to reveal where the money for this would be coming from.

"Out of principle, we should go to court and fight this but sometimes you have to bite your tongue," he said. "We have decided to pay it off in one go to bring an end to this out of court."

A HMRC spokesman declined to comment due to confidentiality issues.

Of course this raised many questions:

'The club is debt free'. So how on earth was the club debt free? Having been hundreds of thousands of pounds owed to creditors it was now debt free!! A year later in 2010 the debt owed to Creditors reappeared at £452K in the Annual Accounts prepared by Mr Razzak. These Accounts did not declare a Turnover figure.

'The £140K debt owed to the Taxman'. In the Accounts it was given as £95K.

There is speculation that Razzak may have been referring to an unpaid Tax bill from the original Basingstoke Town FC Football and Social Club Ltd. It was established that this company did not stop trading until 2005. That is a possible explanation.

It was probably a bit disingenuous of Mr Razzak to imply that the Directors should have shown more diligence in running the finances. Most did not stay at the club for any length of time. From the records at Companies House a staggering 26 Directors joined and left the club. Only Mr Razzak and his CEO David Knight stayed the course. Over the years Rafi Razzak refers to the 'Board'. He was the 'Board'. For Rafi Razzak to view his 'Board' all he had to do was stand in front of a full-sized mirror. Somehow in his mind the problem lay with the Shareholders or the Directors. A new Share Issue was on its way. This time £100 per share. It did draw in a number of new 'Shareholders'. However, it was probably viewed by the new Shareholders more as a donation. One interesting one was Oliver's Fish and Chip Shop at Basing, a very popular establishment in the town. The next big plan was now on its way. This one on the surface did look more credible. A brand new ground at the Old Common, Eastrop. It did court favour with the Council.

So it was 10 years since Rafi Razzak took over as the owner of the club. The ground continued to deteriorate. He was now on another lot of planning and plotting to get into his next target venue.

HM Revenue
& Customs

CHAPTER 11

THE END OF THE SUPPORTERS CLUB

THE CLUBHOUSE END WITH BTG ·

(BEHIND THE GOAL) FANS

The Basingstoke Town Supporters Club contributed much to the club over a very long time. It was said it was the supporters and in particular those from South Ham that helped with funding to build the large stand on the Winchester Road side of the ground. In the last few decades Neil Tysoe and Graham Massey did a sterling job for many years. The John Hacker Stand is believed to have been provided by funds from John Hacker and the Supporters Club. Others who followed also did a good job.

Ian Davies had raised the club profile and John Turner did well to stabilise the ship after Ian Davies departed. Next into the hot seat were the Partridge family. Older supporters would remember the Partridge family as a pop group in the Monkees. This Partridge family had a long association with the club. Ray Partridge was on the Committee for a number of years. His wife June was also very active and a popular figure each week, selling the draw tickets at the gate with Dot Brown. I always joked with June that there should be a prize for the person who bought the most losing draw tickets over the years. After a while I forgot to check them until one week the announcer said two of the three prizes were unclaimed. My younger son Matt thought my numbers may be close and sure enough I had won both prizes. June stayed loyal to the club and was rewarded by being made Patron. However, after a time June stepped down with the parlous state of the Camrose situation.

David Partridge joined as a Director and spent considerable time and effort to progress things. His wife Julie tried to revive the Supporters Club. They were supported by son Graham and daughters Lynda and Diana. David made a good fist of his role at the club and showed energy and interest. Julie introduced small fluffy dolls of Stokie the Dragon. However, like everyone else involved with the club they were forced to give up. The one aspect of countless people who have tried to help the club is the complete lack of any form of appreciation. Hence they become disillusioned and move on. The Partridge family are extremely popular and have a wide network of friends around the town, most especially on Social Media.

In time I was to become firm friends with them. Like me they have now supported Hartley Wintney for a number of years. Our views of Basingstoke Town are identical. In essence they run the club in as shambolic a fashion as possible. Julie has formidable Social Media skills and this has done much to bring the Camrose Scandal to the fore since 2013. They set up a website for the Basingstoke Town Supporters Club. It was re-labelled the Unauthorised Basingstoke Town Supporters Website when they left and it appears on Facebook. I contribute as much as possible to this excellent website.

| John Gray | Rob Paul & Keith Davies |

The division in the fan base continued from 2013 and still exists to this day. Any criticism of the club and you get a torrent of abuse. Essentially some feel we must all be 'Loyalists'. Not to be a 'Loyalist' and you are undermining the efforts to get the club where they want to be. From a personal point of view I do not think I have ever had so much abuse. I have always thought of myself as one of these people that are once met and instantly forgotten. As the Beatles song goes, 'You say hello and I say goodbye!' However, I suppose it is par for the course with Fans' Forums. Not everyone is going to agree on everything. My narrative since 2007 and probably before then was that I wanted Rafi Razzak gone and the Camrose ground brought back up to scratch. Also I wished for professional people to be running the club.

A major problem for the club is that the Clubhouse is outside the ground. The Social Club as such would surely have been better served by being inside the ground or at least accessed from inside the ground like many other clubs. Again, another item on the 'wish list' which did not happen.

Jason Bristow, who had taken over from Frank Gray as manager, was doing well and led the club to a Hampshire Cup Final at Fratton Park – Portsmouth. The opponents were Havant and Waterlooville and it turned out to be a really good match. The Basingstoke support was noisy from the start and saw Manny Williams give them a first half lead. Liam Enver-Marum added a second half goal and it looked like that was that. However, the Hawks fought back and a penalty enabled them to reduce the arrears. Then in the 6th minute of added time they forced in an equaliser from a corner to take the game into extra time. However, it was 'Stoke who scored late on with a fine goal from Liam Enver-Marum two minutes from the end that enabled the Cup to return to Basingstoke. The club finished just below the halfway point in the league but the Hampshire Cup win looked as though it could be the springboard for things to come.

Basingstoke Town had many exceptional supporters over the years. When I first took my sons to the matches we always sat in the Main Stand. There was an elderly gentleman there called Neville. He had a metal cigarette case and he put some coins in the case. When 'Stoke attacked he would rattle the case and shout, 'Heads up – work hard, 'Stoke!!' Or if the other team was attacking it would be, 'Get in their socks, 'Stoke!!' All said in an impeccable Hampshire accent. A true supporter was Dave Stratton. A short man but immensely popular. He was a leader and always seemed to be at the front of a group which usually finished up behind the opponent's goal. Among the group was Greg Ince who still attends the matches. Then there was John Gray, the match day announcer who did much to promote the club in a positive way.

They deserved so much better than what they have been given.

TOWN SUPPORTERS' CLUB IS DISBANDED

By John Boyman

e-mail: john.boyman
@basingstokegazette.co.uk
website:
basingstokegazette.co.uk/sport

AN EXTRAORDINARY General Meeting of the Basingstoke Town FC Supporters' Club has resulted in the organisation being wound up.

A proposal to disband the club was put forward at an open meeting last month and put to a vote at an EGM last week.

Just 12 members attended the meeting and the proposal to wind up the supporters' club was passed unanimously, ending its 60-year history.

Julie Partridge, chairman of the supporters' club's final year, said: "It is a shame. The supporters' club should be there to give fans involvement in the club they support and it's not good when something like that disappears.

"People may start to realise what they had in a few months. We did a lot of publicity on behalf of the club, going to fetes and things."

In the end, it was a lack of interest from everyday sup-

END OF THE ROAD: Julie Partridge, left, and Basingstoke chairman Rafi Razzak.

porters that killed the club – but Partridge believes that the football club could have done more to encourage people to join.

"I do not feel that the club ever saw us as much more than a nuisance and it had

got to the point where it was getting ridiculous," she said. "There was a real them and us mentality.

"The general feeling from fans I have spoken to is that if they are going to pay to join then they want some-

thing in return.

"If nothing is on offer from the club then it is hard to get people to join because they don't feel there is any point."

One thing that attracted people to the supporters' club in the past was discounts on

season and matchday tickets. That perk was stopped a few years ago – something Town chairman Rafi Razzak has defended.

"Our season ticket prices reward loyalty and I don't see why members of the supporters' club should get more of a discount," he said.

"If they are only joining to get a discount on tickets then they are not doing it for the right reasons.

"I do not know why people were not becoming members of the supporters' club.

"Whether they represented the views of supporters, I'm not sure, but it's disappointing that we no longer have a supporters' club.

"I have always thought it is important for supporters to have somewhere to express their feelings about the running of the club and present their views constructively.

"We are grateful for the contribution that the supporters' club has made in terms of running events and raising money for the club.

"However, I have been disappointed because we have not had much put forward to us in terms of views on the running of the club and constructive comments."

JULIE PARTRIDGE

CHAPTER 12

THE NEW STADIUM AT

THE OLD COMMON

PLANS FOR A £10M STADIUM FOR A HAMPSHIRE NON-LEAGUE FOOTBALL CLUB HAVE GONE ON SHOW.

The Annual Accounts were submitted by Rafi Razzak until the final issue in 2018. They showed little in the way of detail and no Turnover figures. They did, however, show a rapidly increasing Creditors' debt which went from £815K in 2012 to around £1.4 million in 2018. The debt appeared to be owed to Mr Razzak. However, he was the owner of the company, declaring the amount of debt owed to himself. Also he was effectively the person who owed the money. In most people's book that would be a balance of zero. The only way these figures can be resolved is for Companies House to get involved and give their verdict. A local Accountant gave a very cautious report on the figures. They did not appear to approve them.

After the debacle with the Down Grange Hub project. Basron put in a bid to build a new Stadium at the Old Common, Eastrop. This one had a better chance at first glance.

Basingstoke Town, which is in the Conference South division, wants to relocate and turn its current ground into a retail park and sports complex.

Club chairman Rafi Razzak said Camrose stadium "falls short of league standards" and the club had "big ambitions for the future club wants to move to land (in red) known as Old Common

The Camrose stadium has a capacity of 2,500 with an average attendance of 312 last season, when the club finished 14th out of 22 teams.

A club spokesman said the new site "would give the club the opportunity to move into a higher league and provide spectators with much improved facilities".

Mr Razzak said: "Camrose has been a fantastic home for us for well over 60 years and it has seen many great sporting moments.

"But now it is in such need of modernising that it threatens to become a major obstacle to realising the club's dreams."

The club wants to use an eight-acre (3.2 hectares) piece of land owned by Basingstoke & Deane Borough Council between London Road and Old Common Road near War Memorial Park. The club said the money for the new stadium, with a planned capacity for 5,124, would come from the sale of the section of the Camrose ground owned by Basingstoke Town.

The plan raised many questions especially in respect to the Lord Camrose Covenant. What had been agreed with the Council? The budgets for the project seemed vague. The Camrose Development plan seemed to indicate that there was to be building on the land owned by the Council.

To the ordinary supporters the issue was still the same. They wanted to stay at the Camrose and see the ground redeveloped. There had been not much apparent consultation with the Board or the supporters to see what their views were. It appeared a plan to enable gain for Mr Razzak. Some said Rafi Razzak was going to pay for most of it in order that he could leave a legacy to the town. Was Razzak going to pay for the stadium with cash up front? Was he going to buy the land at the Old Common or was it to be given to him by the Council?

The doubts were there from the outset. However it was the residents at Eastrop, which is adjacent to the Old Common, who provided the most opposition. They wanted the land to be left as it was and not developed and they made their views known through their local Councillors. It soon emerged that the opposition was beginning to have an impact. Then the news surfaced which probably dismayed Rafi Razzak.

Site for Basingstoke's new football stadium could be reconsidered

Plans to relocate Basingstoke's football stadium face delays after a council U-turn of support last week. At a scrutiny committee of Basingstoke and Deane Borough Council on Thursday, July 24, councillors Stuart Parker and Laura James called for the site location for Basingstoke Town FC's new stadium to be reconsidered.

They warned residents near the new stadium face having their green space downsized.

But councillor John Izett, cabinet member for property, financing and commissioning, warned the U-turn could mean delays of up to five years for the stadium project.

Cllr Izett said: "As a council, we have been in the process of looking at sites since 2009.

"If we are to decide to delay even more and look for another site, it will take even longer to get things done.

"This doesn't send good signals of the borough council as a business partner."

The club wants to upgrade its current Soccer AM Stadium in Western Way to a new 5,124 capacity stadium in Old Common Road, Eastrop. Basingstoke Town FC have previously agreed with the cabinet that the site chosen at Old Common Road will be the best for a new 5,124 capacity stadium.

The opposition was raised because Eastrop councillor Stuart Parker and Norden councillor Laura James said the stadium would cover a third of the land currently used as green space by residents. Clr Parker said: "Insufficient consideration has been given to the potential loss of green open space." It ranks very low on priority by this current administration. "I believe this decision is going against current council policy to protect green space."

Basingstoke Town FC secretary David Knight said: "We feel that there is little more we can do until the cabinet have made up their mind." We will wait until a decision is made."

As a result a public consultation will be launched over August and September for Eastrop residents to give their feedback on the plans.

The Council Meeting in January 2016 saw a considerable number of representations from the Eastrop residents. For Basingstoke Town FC they had just four speakers in favour of the new Stadium at the Old Common. Two of the four were Rafi Razzak and his CEO David Knight. Apart from two supporters no other supporter wanted to speak in favour of the Basron plan.

The Council did not take long to completely reject the plan.

The local press reported:

BASINGSTOKE TOWN FOOTBALL CL

A £10m football stadium will not be built after councillors refused planning permission.

*Non-league Basingstoke Town FC (BTFC) wanted to build the **5,000-capacity ground and training facility** at the town's Old Common.*

Basingstoke and Deane Borough Council said while there were benefits to the stadium, it had become clear the common was well-used.

The club said the rejection was "very disappointing".

*Opponents who had raised concerns about the **loss of open space and the effect on wildlife** staged a protest earlier this month.*

Councillor John Izett said although there were "potentially very significant community benefits in having a football stadium on Old Common", a public consultation on the plans had made it clear there was a "lot of use" of the land.

Chief executive and company secretary of the National League South side, David Knight, said: "The process started 10 years ago and really has been more to the fore in the last three to four years.

"It's a very disappointing decision, not just for the club but for the town as a whole."

Club chairman Rafi Razzak said: "I am extremely disappointed at the decision, having spent so many years believing the council wanted this to happen and working alongside us to achieve what we thought were joint aims."

During the debate on Tuesday evening, 33 people spoke to present their views.

After considering three options, the authority's cabinet voted to "advise BTFC that there is no available or appropriate land in the council's ownership for relocation of the stadium and bring a halt to the current consideration of Old Common, whilst confirming support for BTFC at its current location".

From a supporter's viewpoint this was a mixed blessing. Most wanted to see the Camrose restored to a modern stadium. However, the timescales in chasing after two abortive ground relocations had taken up a lot of time and of course uncertainty. This was 15 years into the Rafi Razzak regime. There was no doubt that Mr Razzak and his CEO David Knight were greatly disappointed. However, what was to come was even worse!!

TALK of the T

Compiled by *The Gazette's* John Boyn

● MOVING ON. David Partridge, left in picture with Chris Fayle, is no longer on the Basingstoke Town FC board.

Partridge hits out at board's "obsession"

FORMER Basingstoke Town director David Partridge has accused the board of being "obsessed" with the club's proposed move to a new ground.

Partridge's exit from the board of directors was announced last Friday after his resignation had been accepted, in his absence, at a meeting the night before.

The announcement came as a surprise to Partridge, who insists that he never formally tendered his resignation. However, he accepts that he announced he was quitting the board at the end of a heated debate with Rafi Razzak before Christmas – words the Town chairman took as an official offer of resignation.

While disappointed to no longer be officially involved with the club he has supported for more than 40 years, Partridge admits that his removal from the board

also came as something of a relief.

"It was like I was banging my head against a wall," he said. "I just felt that I was not being listened to.

"I had ideas to progress the club and bring extra people in but all of them seemed to fall on deaf ears. They did not seem to be given the time of day.

"The big obsession at the moment is the new ground – but that might be years off yet. The club cannot afford to sit back, stagnate and drift along. We have to make the most of what we have got at the moment and push the club forward."

Chairman Razzak refutes the claim that he and the board are focused solely on the new ground project.

"The new ground means a lot to the club going forward, but if it never happens, we have in no way burned all of our bridges," he said.

"We are improving in all areas. Our latest Sports-

man's Dinner was a great success and we launched an on-site Academy last year, which is a big thing for the club. We are also making great strides in getting Basingstoke Town Colts more involved."

Razzak added that he was sorry to see Partridge leave the board. "David Partridge has contributed a lot to the club, as has his whole family," he said. "The club is in debt to anyone who gives as much time as he has and we are sorry to see him go."

Much of the tension between Partridge and the board seems to stem from issues surrounding the refurbishment of the artificial pitches at the Camrose.

With Razzak and the board less than keen to carry out the necessary work, Partridge and an un-named partner took it upon themselves to pay for it to be done more than two years ago.

They planned to get their money back by inviting out-

side agencies to use the facilities – but they are yet to recoup their investment and the details of the agreement have caused numerous problems. However, further discussions have taken place in the last week, resulting in a position that both sides seem to be happy with.

Partridge comes from a family deeply entrenched in Basingstoke Town and his departure from the board has already had a knock-on effect. His wife, Julie, has announced that she is to step down as chairman of the supporters' club in the summer, claiming that her position had been made "untenable" by recent developments.

David Partridge said: "At the moment, I am going to completely breakaway from the club. I have been following Basingstoke Town for 40-odd years, so it's a real shame, but that's not to say that I won't go back again and watch at some point."

DAVID PARTRIDGE

CHAPTER 13

SUCCESS, RONALDINHO AND EBAY

SIMON HOOD (RIGHT)

Basingstoke Town got a boost with the arrival of Simon Hood who joined as a Director. He immediately made a huge effort to raise the profile of the club and one of his first achievements was to entice Soccer AM to show interest. The club re-named the stadium 'The Soccer AM Stadium' for one season. In one of the weeks the show featured Basingstoke Town. This was followed by an audacious effort (probably tongue in cheek) to sign Brazilian International Ronaldinho. It did not happen of course but it attracted interest from the national media.

On the pitch Jason Bristow was proving his worth and the team had an excellent season. The team battled their way through to the FA Cup 1st Round. They were disappointed not to get a league club in the draw but at least they had a winnable home tie. AFC Telford United were the opponents and a decent crowd of around 1,200 turned up on a wet day. 'Stoke had the better of the game and missed some good chances. However, it was Telford who took the lead through a deflected free kick finding the net. Basingstoke pressed non-stop in the second period and finally got rewarded with a Chris Flood equaliser. Try as they could, they could not force a winner. The replay at Telford was always going to be difficult and 'Stoke bowed out with a 2-1 score line.

Off the pitch things were not getting any better as the owner submitted the Annual Accounts to Companies House. The Creditors column just seemed to go up in leaps and bounds. There were no Turnover figures and the amount owed to the Creditors was £1.2 million. For people on the terraces it was difficult to see where all the money was going. The suspicion of course was that the owner was just piling up debt figures to suit his own purpose. Simon Hood was soon to come to the same conclusion as many before him and resigned after a relatively short period of time. Initiatives of the type he had introduced required support. He was clearly not getting it from Basingstoke Town Ltd. To try and draw attention to the club's plight Hood then put the club up for sale on eBay.

The sale of non-league Basingstoke Town on Ebay was "a misguided publicity stunt", according to the club.

The Southern League Premier side were listed on the auction website on Tuesday with bids starting at 99p.

Bidding was suspended by Ebay within the first five hours after reaching £65,900 when a number of high-value offers triggered its security settings.

A new listing has been created, but Basingstoke say creator Simon Hood is "not in a position to sell the club".

Hood, a former director and supporter, told BBC Sport he has had no contact from the club and intends to keep the listing going until bidding closes on 13 December.

Basingstoke Town said the idea of using Ebay to attract new investment has never been discussed.

Basingstoke have played at Camrose Stadium since 1945

*However, **the club statement** applauded "the stunt" for drawing attention to their need to review the Hampshire side's structure with long-standing chairman Rafi Razzak set to step down in May.*

Basingstoke, nicknamed The Dragons and founded in 1896, face an uncertain future at their current Camrose Stadium and have debts of £2m.

*Planning permission for a new 5,000-capacity stadium and training facility on the edge of the town was **refused in January.***

***Mr Razzak was critical of the decision** and admitted his "vision for the club had failed at the local council's hands".*

A year later the Accounts showed an increase in the amount owed to the Creditors at £1.3 million. In most other situations an SME business with such debt would be calling in the Liquidators. However, it appears the FA were happy for the club to carry on in the same parlous way. On the pitch the club progressed to the FA Trophy 1st Round with a win over Whitehawk in the 3rd Qualifying Round. This set up a match against Gosport Borough which ended in a 2-2 draw. The replay saw the teams locked at 1-1 after 90 minutes but it was the Borough who snatched the winning goal to win 2-1 after extra time. Basingstoke Town have never really hit the high spots in this particular competition.

In the League the team were playing attractive football and getting good results. They held their own at the top end of the Division and at times looked as though they may have gained one of the two automatic promotion places. In the end they had to settle for 3rd place and a slot in the playoffs. Whitehawk from Brighton were the opponents and 'Stoke took good support for the away first leg. Chris Flood, a prolific scorer, gave them a first-half lead but they were unable to hold on and the match ended 1-1. The second leg proved to be disappointing and the team were not at their best. Whitehawk won 1-0 and progressed 2-1 on aggregate. However, Jason Bristow could look back on this particular season with some pride. It was probably the highest league position that the club had ever attained. Added to that, the team had reached the 1st Round of the FA Cup.

JASON BRISTOW

CHAPTER 14

THE BIG NAMES ARRIVE

TERRY BROWN

The 2014-2015 season had been an overwhelming success for the club. There was optimism for the next season 2015-2016 under Jason Bristow. Unfortunately the team struggled for form and started to slip down the League. However, they had a good run in the FA Cup and again reached the 1st Round Proper. The draw was probably unkind with an away trip to Cambridge United. In a low key match the Dragons went out to one unopposed goal. The season progressed but the club slipped into the relegation positions. Jason Bristow stepped down as manager and was replaced by his Assistant Manager Michael Gilkes to try and arrest the slide. The former manager being extremely loyal remained at the club to support Gilkes.

Things did not improve and Gilkes was sacked. The replacement for the final matches with relegation all but confirmed was Terry Brown well known in non-league circles. I had watched Terry Brown as a player when he played at Slough Town many years before. He was a decent centre forward and popular with the supporters for his whole hearted commitment. When he moved into management he started at Hayes before moving to Aldershot. At the Shots he had great success over a five-year period and raised the club up the leagues. From Aldershot he moved on to Wimbledon where he again had considerable success taking the club into the Football League. He was sacked from the Dons but is still held in great affection by the Dons supporters to this day. After Wimbledon Terry Brown resurfaced at Margate. I felt this was a strange appointment.

Margate is a fair distance from where Brown lives and works. It did not work out and after a season or so the club and Terry Brown parted company. Now he had the unenviable job of doing something at Basingstoke Town. A Fans Forum was arranged at the end of the season and hearing that the star performer in Rafi Razzak was going to be there, I decided to go. The plan was simple; or something like that! Terry Brown would have Jason Bristow as his second. The club would become a full-time operation based at Alton Town's Anstey Park; the brightest young talent from players released by professional clubs would be recruited. An arrangement with Queen's Park Rangers would be set up. The Forum started with a presentation from the Ark Charity rep. He talked about the amazing work (not disputed) this wonderful charity does. He moved a vote that the stadium be re-named the Ark Charity Stadium which was unanimously carried. I asked a couple of questions relating to the football which were answered by Terry Brown. I had the last question of the evening which I addressed to Rafi Razzak. I asked him what he was going to do about the Camrose Stadium. He refused to answer which was not too surprising. Unknown to me and virtually everyone else at the meeting, he had already purchased the

Ground from Camrose Estates!!

Initially things looked good for the team in the pre-season friendlies. The team won virtually all their matches and played some good football. A very impressive centre back called Rob Atkinson looked as though he could be destined for better things. As soon as the League matches started it became evident that having the younger players may prove to be a problem with the rough and tumble of the Southern League Premier Division. Things picked up after a poor start and generally the team held its own around mid-table. However, they did finish with a bit of success. They saved the best until last and held a very talented Bournemouth Under 21 side to a scoreless draw at Southampton's St Mary's Stadium. Basingstoke triumphed in the penalty shootout to win the Hampshire Senior Cup.

Rafi Razzak announced that he wanted to leave the club. Discussions would take place with an 'Interim Management Group'. The Group was headed up by the Basingstoke Town Club President Alan Turvey. Alan Turvey was certainly a well-known personality in football circles. He had been a referee at the higher levels of football. Once he stepped down he became heavily involved with the Isthmian League. The Isthmian League was generally based around the Greater London area and had some strong clubs as members. The League had previously been Amateur. However, no one really believed they were Amateur and the term 'Sham Amateurism' was often used. Many players for the top sides earned considerable sums of 'boot money' and perks like hire cars.

The Football Association had been effectively a 'closed shop' with non-league clubs trying to gain promotion. The bottom sides in the Football League were always re-elected. The situation started to change when automatic promotion and relegation to the Football League started. Below the Football League the Southern and Northern Leagues introduced promotion and relegation into an Alliance League. The top sides from the Alliance could then go into the Football

League replacing the lowest placed sides. All very well; problem solved, said many. However, the Isthmian League was a powerful league with strong clubs. I can recall Slough Town who were previously an Athenian League side gain promotion to the Isthmian League. Even as an Athenian League side Slough Town had a good support and when paired against Southern League sides usually won.

The Southern League Chairman John Moules of course wanted to preserve the Southern League status and chose to try and fend off the challenge of the Isthmian League clubs in the pecking order. Alan Turvey was having none of it. Under his stewardship the standards of the Isthmian League clubs were brought sharply upwards. The standard of the clubs' play improved and the teams generally played good skilful football. The Southern League sides tended to play a very direct physical game. Alan Turvey and John Moules became bitter rivals as each fought their corners. Turvey eventually got his way and the Isthmian League clubs were brought up to the equal status as their Southern League counterparts. Alan Turvey played a major part in getting Basingstoke Town into the Isthmian League from the Southern League in the late 1980s.

Alan Turvey lived at Basing and I recall him making a speech on the pitch soon after Basingstoke were elected into the Isthmian League. He said that he would not be surprised to see Basingstoke in the Football League within five years. It seemed to inspire the team on that day and they beat Bishop Stortford by 3-1. However, that was as good as it got and the club were relegated at the end of the season.

I had started doing the match reports for Hartley Wintney and enjoying it. It was a help to Graham Merry at the Basingstoke Gazette following the cutting of some staff. One of these was John Boyman who had been a regular contributor on all matters Basingstoke Town. I had known Graham Merry since around 1980, having taught him and his brother how to play chess at Brighton Hill Chess Club.

ALAN TURVEY

I had already started boycotting Basingstoke Town's home fixtures in protest at the awful way the club was being run and the supporters treated following 15 years of Rafi Razzak and things were getting no better. However, I did attend some away fixtures and sent in match reports to the Gazette. At the time they ran a minibus for some away fixtures and I tagged along. The core supporters were usually the ones on the minibus and they were a cheerful bunch especially after they had a drink or two or three even! A considerable number of football fans from Basingstoke travel to non-league grounds elsewhere.

The Camrose ground was effectively finished and needed a massive upgrade. On the Mansfield Road side of the ground some fixings for previous advertising boards looked precarious. The car park was full of potholes. The match experience was just not there despite the best efforts of the club loyalists. Basingstoke Town's relegation was confirmed and new challenges awaited in the Southern League Premier division.

CHAPTER 15

THE BIG PLOT – THE PROTESTS START

If the Town's team's fortunes were not bad enough, despite the Hampshire Cup win, worse was to follow. Basingstoke Town set up an Interim Management Group (IMG) to decide the club's future. Rafi Razzak had decided he wanted out; wanted his money back; and after considering all options wanted to sell the Camrose ground through Basron for development.

The initial IMG group consisted of:

David Knight – Chief Executive and Company Secretary

Alan Turvey – Chairman (Club President)

Terry Brown – First Team Manager

Steve Williams – Strategy and Projects

Will Wilkinson – Digital and Marketing

Mark Jones – Ark Charity (Non-Executive Director)

Mark Lane – Accountants (Finance)

Ian Halloway – Stadium Operations and Safety

Sarah Parsons – Events and Hospitality

James Mathie – Community Club Advisor

At a meeting between the above and Councillor Simon Bounds the Councillor expressed an opinion the club should remain at the Camrose ground. There were no other locations for an alternative football ground in Basingstoke.

However, the IMG group felt they had little option but to accept that Mr Razzak's wishes were to be honoured and relayed that to Councillor Bounds. For the forthcoming season the club were to be moved to Farnborough Football Club to play for a season. Basron the Developers would fully fund this move and after that the provisional plan was to move to Whitchurch. Mr Razzak is understood to have offered around £250K as an ongoing payment. Also he would wipe out all debts. Councillor Bounds seems to have been convinced that a presumption based on the above was the only way forward. This presumption would have meant the loss of one of the town's two main football arenas.

This was of course unacceptable most especially as it was well known the Lord Camrose Covenant covered the ground lease until 2053. This should have been protecting the ground. Most thought that surely the Council would scupper this outrageous and audacious action.

The Protesters started their quest to mobilise the opposition. Simon Hood, who had previously been a member of the Basingstoke Town Board, was at the forefront of the initial effort. Simon had made a name for himself in his excellent efforts to promote the club. Simon

Hood was soon to be joined by the Partridge family. While running the Supporters Club the Partridges had set up an impressive website for the club. Once they left their roles this website was rebranded as 'The Unauthorised Basingstoke Town FC' site. This site subsequently proved to be very effective especially in the 2019 protests. Julie's skills on the website were considerable and clearly highlighted a definite loss to Basingstoke Town FC.

The announcement to move to Farnborough had to be opposed in my opinion. I felt strongly that I should get involved. Simon Hood set up a group called 'KFIB' – 'Keep Football In Basingstoke'. A petition drew 700 signatures. The final scheduled match at the Camrose brought in a crowd of 700. There were protests on the pitch as well as fans chaining themselves to the goalposts.

I went along to the Business Expo at the Apollo Hotel in Basingstoke. This was an event for local businesses Simon Hood, who organised the protest, was there along with David Partridge and Martin French. Martin was trying to revive and start a new Supporters Club. A few other fans came along. I had put together a display board with pictures of a number of famous matches in the past which seemed to attract attention. We set it up at the entrance to the hotel with approval from the Apollo Management.

During the day the hotel kindly offered the occasional coffee and were supportive of our efforts. I managed to engage quite a number of interested businesspeople and all were supportive of our initiative in keeping football in the town. A number were previously involved with the club but had since become detached for a variety of reasons. Most were very disparaging towards Mr Razzak. Simon Hood went into the main exhibition hall and came out with a huge number of signatures and offers of support. I was expecting some from Rafi Razzak's circle of friends to come to where we were based at the front of the hotel. Sure enough, on cue a gentleman from a local charity showed up. He said, 'You are wasting your time!! The club will definitely be playing at Farnborough next season.' Regarding the Covenant he said that it was no longer legally valid. I got around 36 signatures and Simon Hood in the Exhibition Hall many more.

Overall I thought the effort at the Expo was worth it. I met a few nice fans who I had not previously met. I agreed with Simon Hood and David Partridge that a completely new club was certainly the best way forward. Perhaps a ground share at somewhere like Overton or the HFA Headquarters at Winklebury. Start at the very bottom and begin working up. Basingstoke Town were finished as the club we had identified with. It was now a complete shambles.

A few weeks later a Fans' Forum was organised at the Camrose. I did not intend to go until it was announced that Rafi Razzak would be there. He was going to answer the questions. On the day of the meeting it was announced that the club were to continue playing at the Camrose ground for the forthcoming season. The meeting attracted a big attendance including two Councillors, Simon Bounds and Sean Keating. Alan Turvey was Chairman for the meeting and the first question came from Ian Davies. Razzak looked down and said, 'Can I have another question?'

A second question was delivered and then another but none answered. At this point I said to Alan Turvey, 'Mr Chairman, is it possible that Mr Razzak could actually answer some questions!'

Razzak moved into familiar territory saying how he had a vision for the club and he would always make sure it was 'debt free'. The Councillors spoke but their content was difficult to comprehend. A chap from a firm which sets up Community Clubs did a good talk. The meeting seemed to conclude and I intended to finish my drink and go. Mr Razzak had gone, or so we thought. All of a sudden he came rushing back into the room and said he would give the club £250K. Of course this meant nothing to my aspirations for the club's future. I was thinking at least 10 times that value would have been more appropriate for the Camrose.

Simon Hood went to the Council and outlined the protesters' grievance. The Councillors said they were totally sympathetic with the fans and stated the importance of football to the town. In other words, all the usual platitudes.

Several weeks later I received a call from Alan Turvey. It was pleasant enough but we were on two differing wavelengths. Alan felt that unity was a must in dealing with Rafi Razzak. He had known him for years and he was really not such a bad guy. We talked about the Covenant and he said it was no longer valid. Unfortunately it probably had been lost years ago. He asked if he could have a meeting with David Partridge and myself. He phoned back later and asked if David Knight could come along. I said I had no objections. I sorted out a room at the Bridge and Chess Club and Martin French was also invited.

With David Knight present I could not see the meeting lasting very long. I went in with the Che Guevara approach. Guevara was a Cuban Revolutionary who came up with a few good expressions. The one I was going to use was, 'Be a realist! Ask for the impossible!!' The impossible I outlined at the start which was that David Knight should resign. Obviously this was unacceptable and the meeting lasted just five minutes with no agreement.

A month or so later the Big Plot was announced at the Council Chambers. Alan Turvey presented the outline details which were:

- Basingstoke Town will move to Winklebury.

- They will share the Hampshire FA headquarters with the Hampshire FA.

- A new Community Club will be formed to run the affairs of Basingstoke Town FC. This club will be fully democratic. One member, one vote.

- The Camrose ground can then be redeveloped.

Excellent presentations were made by David Partridge, giving the viewpoint of the KFIB protesters at three Council meetings. After the Council meeting I spoke with Councillor Simon Bounds. I provided him with an article detailing the history of the Camrose ground. I also discussed the best way to deal with an effective land grab. It certainly is not to leave the ground; most especially if you are the Leaseholder and the Council. With hindsight I would probably have had more success speaking to the man on the moon.

KFIB – THE FANS PROTEST – 2017

CHAPTER 16

QUEST TO SAVE A FOOTBALL CLUB –

I HAD PREVIOUS

BENBURB FC LEGEND TOMMY DOUGLAS –
SIR ALEX FERGUSON AND MYSELF
SIR ALEX IS IN THE MIDDLE

In recent years I have come to the conclusion that I put the kybosh on teams that I support. Now actively involved in trying to preserve both the town's two main football arenas, I had previously been involved in trying to save a football club.

I was brought up in Govan, a Burgh in Glasgow. It is famous for its shipbuilding industry as well as producing many good footballers. Also famous for comedian Rab C. Nesbitt. Kenny Dalglish spent a time in Govan and Gordon Brown, the former Prime Minister, was born there. However, he never mentions it!! Rangers were the team I supported as the local senior football team in Govan. Below Rangers there were two Junior Clubs in the Burgh. One was St Anthony's who played in green and white hoops and attracted a number of Celtic fans to their matches. However, it was the other that I fell in love with and it was a team called Benburb FC. Their nickname was 'the Bens' and they played in blue. This linked them to the Rangers. In Scotland Junior football in the 1950s was extremely popular. The term 'Junior' meant they were effectively the non-league of Scotland. Many of the teams were very strong and could probably have competed in the Scottish Senior Leagues. Benburb attracted big crowds and a ground record at their huge Tinto Park was set in 1953 when 20,000 attended a Scottish Junior Cup match.

In 2000 I had driven up to Scotland with Sue to see Benburb play a Junior Cup semi-final against Whitburn at Airdrie. They lost on penalties after a 1-1 draw and extra time. They should have won having been the better side virtually throughout. However, it was not to be and they had to satisfy themselves with the League title and also the League Cup.

Three years later the club were in desperate trouble and the predictions were they were unlikely to survive. Their Tinto Park ground had been vandalised and they were playing all their matches away. It was not a scandal but a situation far worse than that which currently faces Basingstoke Town. The Social Club was understood to have been taken over by a drug gang and they were involved in a vicious turf war with another gang.

I had been pretty devastated at the thought of the club being lost and wondered what I could do to help. With the club homeless and virtually penniless things were bleak. However, the Club Committee were not for giving up. I decided to produce their matchday programmes through my business and send them up to Govan for the home matches. My eldest son Stuart set up a website for them and at least we were making a contribution which was greatly appreciated. This was to last 10 years. No sooner than we had got involved at the club, disaster struck. At a popular Curry and Pint event at the Social Club someone involved in the drug war was stabbed to death. This led to a high-profile trial where the verdict against the accused came back as 'Not Proven'. Undaunted and with remarkable resilience, the Committee somehow managed to get the pitch playable again and home matches were again being staged at a very crumbling Tinto Park ground. A further setback came along when possibly in some sort of revenge attack the Social Club was burned down. This turned out in some ways to be a positive. Many Govanites who were former Benburb supporters from all over the world sent in contributions which kept the club afloat. I decided to send a programme to Sir Alex Ferguson, the Manchester United manager. Sir Alex had been a keen Benburb fan throughout his life. When he is asked what is the first result he looks for in Scotland he always says, 'It is not Rangers. It is not Celtic. It is not Aberdeen. It is Benburb Football Club!!'

Alex Ferguson was born very near to where I lived in Govan, a stone's throw from the 50 pitches on Shieldhall Road. I had seen him at the Bens matches with his dad who was also a supporter. Latterly he had gone to the matches with his friends. Virtually by return of post I received a reply from Sir Alex. I had explained the situation to him and like me he was concerned about the state of the club. He immediately offered to help in any way he could and that help was to last for 10 years from 2003 to 2013. He offered financial help from Trusts that he had set up for Govan projects in memory of his mother. In addition, he provided articles for the programme. Of course with Sir Alex involved the morale of the Bens committee rose sky high and strengthened their resolve to survive. There was not a lot that could be done in respect to the team. The new Co-Managers Frank Lovering and Dennis Donnelly had called it 'Mission Impossible'. Benburb were to tumble all the way down to the bottom league with a series of straight relegations.

The one thing that everyone at the club agreed on without exception was the need to stay playing at Tinto Park until a solution to the many problems could be overcome. This is the normal approach in the UK by clubs trying to survive when their ground is threatened. When a club loses its ground it very often finishes up becoming Defunct. Sir Alex was a total inspiration to the club followers. When the club had a big cup match he would phone up first thing on a Monday and find out the score and who scored. Also what was happening at the club; he wanted to be kept informed. He always said he enjoyed reading the programmes in particular of times past.

After a few years things at the club began to stabilise. However, then there was a setback when the Committee had a disagreement on the way forward. There were two conflicting views. Both groups agreed that the ground needed to be sold to pay off debts and both agreed that the likely destination of the new ground was acceptable. However, they did not agree on who the Builder should be and who the Developer should be. Both offered good options and when it came to the vote both parties were equally divided in numbers. It was left to the Club President Tommy Douglas to have the casting vote and he opted for the proposal put forward by Frank Lovering. The other group were not happy and sadly left the club which was unfortunate. The entire committee had performed an amazing feat to keep the club afloat. Tommy Douglas was an icon at Benburb, having been at the club for 60 years in just about every capacity. Alex Ferguson always said he was his favourite ever Benburb player.

In 2010 Sir Alex contacted me to ask if he could come to Govan and spend an evening at the club. This was duly accepted!! It was a late autumn evening and the Benburb committee were excited when he arrived. It was an evening none of us were to forget, of course, as Sir Alex recalled his time supporting the club. He was delighted to meet once again with the club legend Tommy Douglas. He was shown a picture of a 1950s team and amazingly was able to pick out a number of the players by name. He asked to be shown the pitch. He went out onto the pitch and gave his compliments to the groundsman on such a fine surface. The only light coming on to the pitch was from the clubhouse. I asked club secretary Archie Wiseman if he could turn on the floodlights. Archie replied, 'Sorry David!! Someone got into the ground yesterday and stole all the cable to the floodlights.' Down each side of the pitch were trenches where the cables had been buried. Sir Alex talked about everything being totally at home with his fellow Govanites. He recalled his last match at the 50 Pitches. He said it was an evening match in late season. 'When we returned to the changing rooms it was dark as the daylight had almost gone. The changing rooms had no lights and the only water was a cast-iron drinking fountain at the entrance to the pitches. This was used to wash out the gravel from the mainly ash pitches.' Sir Alex continued, 'We went in and there was a huge pile of clothes. When I came out I realised I had come out with someone else's underpants on!!' At the end of the evening he asked to see me privately and to my astonishment gave a huge donation to the club and asked to be continually kept informed.

A truly remarkable man who never forgot his roots.

In 2013 it was announced that Benburb Football Club would be leaving their Tinto Park ground where they had played since 1933. The ground was to be sold for a housing development Their new home was right behind Tinto Park and was to be called New Tinto Park. They played one season away while the new ground was built and returned 'home' to Govan in 2015. Since moving into their new ground the Bens have climbed back up the leagues and now compete in the top Division again.

When Sir Alex last went up to Govan he drove around the new housing estate where the ground was. He said somehow he felt sad. The ground had provided such nostalgic memories of the past.

With the experience of the Benburb Football Club affair I hoped to help the KFIB and others in their efforts with Basingstoke Town. To the football fraternity, football grounds are important to many aspects of their life. Something that some people in Basingstoke should reflect on before giving away the town's main football arena.

TINTO PARK – BENBURB FC

CHAPTER 17

THE COMMUNITY CLUB STARTS

HAMPSHIRE FA HEADQUARTERS – WINKLEBURY

A Council meeting in July 2017 was well attended by many club supporters. I was hoping to make a presentation. I had previously been told by Councillor Simon Bounds that I was unlikely to be able to speak as I did not represent anyone. Apparently it was 50 signatures that were required. I set up a Temporary Supporters Group and within nine days without much effort achieved the required number. I ensured that all were associated with Basingstoke Town and not names plucked out of a telephone book. Before the meeting I asked Councillors Bounds and Harvey if I could speak. Both approved and I got my two minutes of fame. I emphasised the importance of the Covenant and the fight to try and stay at the ground. I paid tribute to the loyal support given by Micky Stevens and Martin French to the club. At the end of my two minutes of fame I did say I did not support the Community Club.

David Partridge was allotted four minutes and gave a very professional presentation below:

David Partridge – Submission for report – Basingstoke Town Football Club Community, Environment and Partnerships Committee 19th July 2017

The following is submitted for information and discussion.

While both the IMG and Supporters are in agreement that the way forward is the setting up of a new Community Club to take over ownership of Basingstoke Town Football Club, many supporters remain frustrated by the apparent acceptance of those on the IMG of the "done deal" and lack of challenge to it. Mr Razzak has taken our club, our ground, and threatened our future, and we feel very strongly that, alongside the need to find a way forward, there are four basic areas within BTFC that still need urgently to be addressed.

1. Lord Camrose Covenant. We know from research, from knowledge handed down from those who were here at the time, and from documentation held at the Land Registry, that the Camrose Ground land was given to the people of Basingstoke (original lease held by aldermen of the borough and then the Basingstoke Corporation) on a 99-year lease, for the use of sport. Date: 12 November 1953, Term: 99 years from 24 June 1953. Rent: A peppercorn. Parties: (1) The Right Honourable William Ewert Viscount Camrose and The Right Honourable Mary Agnes Viscountess Camrose (2) Cyril Wood and Frank Spencer Spurling. Date: 17 May 1962, Term: 92 years from 30 June 1960. Rent: £65. Parties: (1) The Basingstoke Corporation (2) Cyril Wood and Harold Redstall Basron.

Mr Razzak and Mr McPhail now own the land but it has not been confirmed that the covenant is no longer valid – again, research at the Land Registry reveals that the transfer of land is still subject to this covenant (21.07.2016). The Transfer to the proprietor contains a covenant to observe and perform the covenants by the landlord contained in the lease dated 12 November 1953 referred to in the Charges Register and of indemnity in respect thereof. We believe that if Mr Razzak & Mr McPhail are indeed to build on the Camrose land then another piece of land should be provided by them for the club to continue with the terms of the original lease until at least June 2052 and they should give a proper explanation of exactly what they intend to do about this.

2. The Golden Share. This refers to a preference share put in place when Basingstoke Town Ltd was formed in 2001, taking over from the former company, Basingstoke Town Football & Social Club Ltd when that company went into administration. As stated in the gazette article of that year:

http://www.basingstokegazette.co.uk/news/5615895.Town_s____1m_share_b id/ and another of 2007 during a later share issue:

http://www.basingstokegazette.co.uk/news/1167809.Buy_a_share_in_the_fut ure/ this is a single £5000.00 share, registered on documents held at Companies House, that prevents the club from being taken over 100% by any one person, and is designed to protect the club, ground and land at The Camrose, making sure the land remains in operation for football use.

Mr Razzak claimed at the recent fans forum that this share was lost when the club went into administration but this can't be the case because this share was put in place by Mr Razzak at the formation of the new company. We believe that Mr Razzak misled the members in 2001, is relying on people not challenging him regarding the intended purpose of this share, and should give a proper explanation of what he has done with it.

3. The Fanbase. Many people have stepped up from the Fanbase to try to move things forward over many years, but not one of them has managed to break through and make any difference, as Mr Razzak has consistently refused to listen, or to properly invest either on or off the field And despite never having wanted to put any of his own money in to the club he has actively blocked every opportunity for community involvement or outside investment, and he has quite recently stated on local radio that he does not believe the community model will work. He has never involved anyone at the club in any of his plans, including

those for the move to Down Grange or Old Common, which had no input at all from either the Board of Directors or Supporters Representatives, and so the club has lurched on from one crisis to the next, one set of directors and volunteers to another, until finally we are where we are. The Fanbase does not feel included or part of the club, feels left out of the discussion, is a very frustrated body, and supporters have dealt with this in differing ways. Some still continue to attend home games to support the squad, some attend away games only, to support the squad while not putting any further money in at home, and a good number do not attend at all, stating they will not set foot in the place again while Razzak is still in any way involved. All of these supporters need to feel that they are able to come together to support the new community club, but there is great concern that Mr Razzak's continued involvement, his refusal to answer the questions, and the uncertainty surrounding his intended departure, will be detrimental to this.

4. The Debt. Fans are extremely concerned about statements made by Mr Razzak regarding his "loans", clearing the "debt", setting a "self-sustaining budget". Mr Razzak states that he will, on being granted planning permission, transfer a minimum sum of £250,000 to the Community Club. We believe too much attention has been focussed on keeping Mr Razzak sweet in order that this money will be forthcoming – we are told we "should not upset Mr Razzak" – but planning permission could take months, years even, considering at the moment no application has even been submitted. Supporters are also asking "do we have that in writing?" Mr Razzak states that he will ensure the new club is "debt free".

The concern is that he will again use a CVA to achieve this, as he did with the setting up of Basingstoke Town Ltd, when many local businesses, as well as the council, who were owed money by the previous company, lost out. The club has struggled for many years with businesses as well as supporters refusing to put money into the club because of this, and there is great concern that the new Community Club could suffer through more bad feeling in the town if this were to happen again. Mr Razzak is unable to state how much he expects to reclaim as monies owed to him from the sale of our ground. He is unable to put a value on the land or a figure on the amount of profit he hopes to make. We believe that if the land is to be sold, then BTFC should see some benefit from this sale just as

Mr Razzak and Centerprise have benefitted from their involvement in BTFC. We believe that Mr Razzak should give a proper explanation of the finances involved both in the land deal and the transfer of ownership of BTFC to the new Community Club.

In conclusion, whatever happens regarding the setting up of a community club, the most important thing we need is a ground, a stadium to play in, a home. In general, most fans would prefer to stay at the Camrose, our home, and essentially we ask for the council's help to do this. What we as supporters would like to ask of the council is that BDBC look seriously at the proposal which was raised at the forum, to purchase the 71% of the Camrose Land now owned by Basron, so taking over the entire site, and lease it back to the new Community Football Club. This would provide a return on the purchase through rental income and in the long term, should the launch of the community club fail, would see BDBC owning the land, which could then be used as they saw fit. Alan Turvey, the current club president, has already looked into a development proposal to turn the ground around and partially develop for housing to raise money to redevelop the stadium. Looking into this would give BDBC an immediate return on at least part of their investment. There are several models of community owned clubs, who run community services on behalf of their local council and/or have purpose built stadia built by their local council, which could be studied, and it is worth noting that a community owned club, as opposed to a private limited company, would be able to apply for development and community grants to carry out much of the needed recovery of the club.

A discussion followed on the Covenant. The Council advised that the Covenant was 'lost'!! The fact that it was on the Land Registry document in 2016 did not seem to matter. Without seeing the original document nothing could be done.

FROM THE COUNCIL MINUTES: 19th JULY 2017

♣ Uncertainty around the covenant on the land upon which the football club ground was sited which restricted its future development potential.

♣ Uncertainty regarding the 'golden share' that was supposed to protect the club and the ground.

The committee considered the report and the contributions made by visiting speakers. The discussion covered the following areas:

♣ Concern that Basingstoke and Deane Borough Council were having difficulty in locating the covenant documentation relating to the Camrose site, given that the authority owned 29% of the site.

Undaunted, Alan Turvey gave details which I thought were vague. The Community Club were to represent the views of the football fraternity whether you joined it or not. Mr Razaak and Basron were home and dry.

The July 2017 meeting at the Council signalled the start of the Community Club. Steve Williams was charged with setting it up and he started with enthusiasm. The new Community Club leader had previously been at Basingstoke Town some years before both as a player and also as a manager. The tenure as manager was relatively short as he moved out the area after around one season. In that season he had done well with a very low budget and against predictions of relegation the club had survived.

However, his appointment was completely at cross purposes for what the KFIB (Keep Football in Basingstoke) were trying to achieve. Most who supported the protests wanted to stay at the Camrose ground. If not then a new ground in Basingstoke. The proposition of going to Winklebury could only ever be a temporary home while the new ground was being built. At least that is what we understood. However, the new ground was not mentioned and the Council, with Councillor Simon Bounds leading, appeared set in offering the Hampshire FA complex at Winklebury as the only option. There being little effective opposition like ourselves, it was difficult trying to deflect either the Council or the Community club away from this quest. However, the feeling was that it would surface at some time in the form of a Planning Application. Then the Covenant would be raised and Objections would surely be put forward. Sport England were also likely to ask for the One-for-One replacement also known as a Section 106 replacement.

Most of the people at our side of the debate could not believe what was happening. Surely the Council would do some research into what they were doing!! As it turned out they were not and went along with the Alan Turvey plan to move to Winklebury. As someone who follows the situations with football grounds I had assumed the figure of £250K must be a mistake. Possibly they meant £2.5 million with a decimal point misplaced. We could only wait and bide our time.

Steve Williams started setting up his Board and was joined by Steve Letch, a very popular supporter. A massive recruitment drive was made to recruit members and had some success. To outsiders like me and others the Community Club fell over at the first hurdle. When it was set up the feeling was they had to have total control of the club, including the Clubhouse. Alas, this did not happen. This was an important revenue stream. Also, the existing Basingstoke Town Ltd retained all the matchday money. Add to that, and the Community Club had to raise the funds to play the players' wages. It was already all but dead in the water and that was before they had elected a single officer as we had seen it.

The season started reasonably but the FA Cup exit to Hartley Wintney was a bitter pill to swallow. Steve Williams tried to build bridges with the Winklebury Community but we understand the response was lukewarm. I have nothing but respect for Steve Williams and Steve Letch; they were on a Mission Impossible with Basron and Basingstoke Town Ltd calling all the shots. Martin French joined the Board and his hard work certainly made a huge difference and still does. With a lot to cope with and little reward the Board members started to drift off after a relatively short time.

Councillor Bounds then started setting up agreements with the Hampshire FA in respect to some form of collaboration. Alan Turvey spoke about this at the Council meetings. It seemed a big agreement between the political parties, the Community Club and the Council, the Basingstoke IMG (Interim Management Group) and the Hampshire Football Association. In essence as I saw it 'All Jolly Guys Together'. A football equal to David Cameron's big society. It was a total farce with Councillor Bounds setting up all sorts of complex agreements as should have been anticipated with such a collaboration.

The departure of Steve Letch left a huge void, not least because he was recognised as being a keen fan with a good grasp on business matters. Terry Brown who had several different roles at the club on the Playing side eventually took over as Chairman. The Community Club Board and Admin started to have the look of the original Board, mainly because nobody would put their name forward to serve. Some felt that the club had been run down and somehow the burden of restarting would fall on willing people but without the certainty of having a recognised home ground. Last year (2019) Kevin White joined as Vice Chairman. Like Terry Brown he was of the opinion that the Winklebury complex was the only realistic option. They were well aware that there was a strong body of opinion suggesting that the club should move back to the Camrose or if not a One-for-One replacement should be provided.

In the early part of 2019 the Community Club advised that the club would be moving into Winklebury for the 2019-2020 season and sold season tickets at £99 each. Around 150 fans bought the tickets. Work had already been budgeted for by the Hampshire FA to provide a 3G surface as well as other improvements at Winklebury and these went ahead. Some additional work was funded on a small scale to help a possible Basingstoke Town FC move. However, to get the ground approved for the Southern League an FA inspection is required by March each year. The Winklebury Complex was a long way short of the requirements.

The last match was played at the Camrose against Taunton Town and ended in a 2-1 defeat. This meant relegation for the club into the Southern League South-West Division. The Community Club then went into a ground share at Winchester City, claiming they were evicted. This was not strictly true. The club Basingstoke Town Ltd was owned by Mr Razaak who had 100% of the shares. He moved his club to Winchester City. After several days the club transferred the license to operate as Basingstoke Town to the Community Club.

They market themselves as 'The Oldest-New Club in England'. Of course they cannot be both. If it is the old club then they are leaving at least £1.4 million worth of debt. If it is a new club then why should they have been treated differently from any other new club? Of course it is still effectively the 'old' club with many of the original people clambering back on board.

I have had contact indirectly and directly with members of the Board and told them that I feel they should abandon the Winklebury quest. However, they still persist going along this avenue at this moment in time.

The split in the fan base has not helped the Community Club. They derive most of their support from the Camrose Clubhouse and could be described as 'Loyalists'. Many others including myself believe a new ground to replace the Camrose is essential and Winklebury is not that answer. When the KFIB (Keep Football in Basingstoke) was launched in the 2017 protests there was not universal support from the Loyalists. It was left to the KFIB to organise the protests which gathered in 700 signatures on a petition to avoid the move to Farnborough. The re-run in February 2020 of the protests produced a similar pattern. With a petition of 'Save the Camrose – No to Winklebury' two petitions drew 2,500 signatures. The Loyalists believe the saving of the club is important. KFIB believe it is more important to save the ground in the form of a One-for-One replacement for the Camrose. In our eyes the move to Winklebury favours Mr Razzak and Basron.

COUNCILLOR SIMON BOUNDS

CHAPTER 18

BASINGSTOKE CHALLENGERS –

PAST AND PRESENT

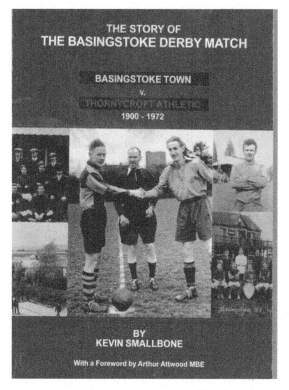

EXCELLENT LOCAL PUBLICATION FROM KEVIN

SMALLBONE PRODUCED IN 2020

HIGHLY RECOMMENDED

THORNEYCROFTS ATHLETIC FC

Nowadays within the Borough of Basingstoke there is only one club. Several of the outlying villages have teams but within the borders give or take three miles there is only team. That team is Basingstoke Town FC.

However, it was not always the case. For 60 years prior to 1972 there was a good local rivalry between Basingstoke Town and Thorneycroft Athletic. Thorneycrofts were a big employer in the town in the early part of the 20th Century, making trams and motor vehicles. They had a ground at West Ham near where the Thorneycroft roundabout is now. The rivalry between Thorneycrofts Athletic and Basingstoke Town attracted big crowds with the matches played over Bank Holidays. In its heyday the Thorney's could attract good players by offering them employment at their factory. For the period up to 1950 both clubs shared an equal number of wins against one another. Even beyond then there were a number of close matches before the factory went into decline before disappearing. Several of the officials including the well-known Neil Kimber moved to Basingstoke Town, as did most of the support.

RS BASINGSTOKE

In 1971 the Soldiers Return pub had a team which started showing ambition. Having done well in the Basingstoke League they wanted to move up the pecking order. They joined and left a good number of leagues over the years. Starting at the Chiltonian League, they had spells in the Combined Counties League, Hampshire League, North Hants League and Hellenic League. They changed their name to DCA Basingstoke when Danesmead Community Association became sponsors. Finally it was RS Basingstoke after the Railway Social became sponsors. The club were reasonably successful throughout their history and picked up the odd league title and cup. The disadvantage they had was the ground. Whiteditch on Sherborne Road was effectively an open playing field with one changing room block. They could not collect a gate income. However, they were a well-run club that surely deserved more support than what they got. The matches I watched at Whiteditch always seemed to result in a win for the Basingstoke team. Sadly the club folded in 2005.

AFC BASINGSTOKE FC

A more short-lived side but also with a bit of ambition was AFC Basingstoke which was formed in 1993. They started as the George after the George pub at the top of town. They quickly progressed through the local leagues and finished up in the Hampshire League. They were required to have floodlights so they played their fixtures at Portals between Overton and Whitchurch. The club hoped to move into Basingstoke and applied to have a ground at the east end of Down Grange. Unfortunately the Council turned the club down.

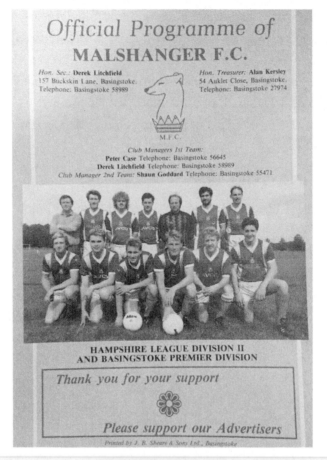

MALSHANGER FC

Malshanger village is near Oakley. The team evolved from the local Basingstoke Sunday League and did well to rise into the Hampshire League. They were successful and won a number of the local cups. Obviously as Malshanger is a tiny village their draw of support was always going to be small. However, they produced a good matchday programme for the 40 or 50 who watched them play. After finishing bottom of a Hampshire League Division and an exodus of players they folded in 1997.

OVERTON UNITED FC

OVERTON UNITED

A long established local village club and always noted as being competitive. The home venue is the picturesque Bridge Street ground. Very tightly packed in around the village centre and the adjacent church makes a lovely backdrop. The club still thrives and plies their trade in the Hampshire League.

WHITCHURCH UNITED

I have attended many games at Whitchurch over the years. The Longmeadow ground is a decent standard for the level they play at. The most notable feature of the pitch is the large slope from one end to the other. The club never seem to attract much in the way of support and do well to maintain the Wessex League level. Over the years they bounce up and down between the two Wessex League Divisions.

TADLEY CALLEVA

Tadley is a decent sized village and the club seem to get decent support at their Barlow's Park ground. They have made a steady progress up the divisions from local football and have now reached the Wessex Premier Division where they are holding their own. Tadley do have the potential for good support as demonstrated when they played Basingstoke Town in 2014 in the Hampshire Cup. They had several hundred cheering them on to a win on penalties after a 2-2 draw. They have a decent policy of ongoing improvements at their ground.

Apart from Thorneycroft Athletic, Basingstoke Town has not had an alternative club to give them a challenge for the football business in the town. Competition is healthy and it gives the paying public a choice. An ideal situation would be Basingstoke Town playing at Conference level and an alternative side in Basingstoke playing at Wessex League level within the town. On present trends if the situation continues we could have just the one side playing at Wessex League level. This is due to the fallout from the Camrose Scandal.

The attitude taken by the club over many years seems to be: 'Well, there it is – take it or leave it !!' Of course the vast bulk choose the latter and leave it. To be successful any football club at non-league level must provide a good matchday experience. Good value at a decent price. Basingstoke Town have always been at the high end of the entrance fee. They charge for Car Park and Transfer to Stand when most clubs do not. It is apparent that the ground became 'not fit for purpose'.

CHAPTER 19

THE COMPETITION ARRIVES –

HARTLEY WINTNEY FC

photo: Paul Paxford

With the situation at Basingstoke Town seemingly in a permanent downward spiral of despair, I had been watching more and more games elsewhere. As illustrated previously my feeling was that unfortunately Basingstoke Town did not have enough competition locally. Hence the competition to Basingstoke Town was from further outside the town. Without competition of course they could carry on in much the same vein as before. The club officials, however well-meaning and efficient were hampered by an owner who rarely made a sensible decision to the benefit of football.

However, competition was about to arrive from up the A30. The club which had the most potential was Hartley Wintney FC. I had watched a couple of matches there prior to 2004. However, the Sunday team in which my sons Stuart and Matt played called Jasmine's Heroes, reached the Final of one of the Hampshire Sunday Cups. The venue was Hartley Wintney. Prior to the game my sons asked me to be the manager for the night. The usual manager was a player manager and it only needed a couple of people to sit on the bench. I had been volunteered and a chap called John was to be the sponge man. John arrived at the touchline with his bucket of water with sponge and put it down. After that I did not see him again. Fortunately there were no serious knocks. It was a decent match won by a team called Sandrock by 5-3. After the match the Hartley Wintney club put on sandwiches and refreshments for all the players and officials. Prior to the match they had also produced a programme for the fixture. This impressed me greatly, most especially their friendliness. I made a point of watching them at least a few times each season.

Most seasons tended to be either a promotion push from the lower of two Combined Counties League, or if they did get promoted a struggle to avoid relegation from the Premier League. The crowds seemed to range from 40 to 60. In general Hartley Wintney do seem to be a competitive village when it comes to sports. Their cricket team do well locally and on a consistent basis. The village where I live at Kempshott does not have a football team and as far as I am aware does not have a cricket team. Of course sports players in Kempshott play for other clubs in Basingstoke. However, the feeling you get is that the Council and Kempshott in particular have very little interest in sport.

One feature I liked at Hartley were the hanging baskets along the veranda. On a sunny day what could be better than having a drink and standing or sitting on the veranda? I felt looking out over the field that it was football in an English country garden. This of course a far cry from my childhood days. We played on ash parks mostly at the 50 pitches in Govan. No nets, corner posts and very faint touchlines. The only water available was from a cast-iron fountain drinking well where you pressed the button for water. This was usually used to clean the grazes from the ash inflicted after the falls.

The changing rooms were unlit and small. Sir Alex Ferguson was born very near to the 50 pitches.

A far cry from Hartley Wintney whose nickname is 'The Row'. The club had a good fighting spirit which reminded me a bit of my other team from years gone past, Benburb FC. They often had a different sort of fighting spirit!! At Tinto Park they had placed the dugouts on the opposite side of the pitch after some scraps on the touchline between the managers.

The Row were developing a good team by the time 2015-16 came along. Two new managers, Dan Brownlie and Anthony Millerick, had arrived and both showed much enthusiasm. The team seemed to gel instantly and having taken over the duties as a match reporter I seemed to be reporting wins every week. The team spirit was apparent and the fitness levels very high. The side looked strong in all departments. They carried a big threat with their two main strikers, Sam Argent and Ross Cook. Argent was a natural goal scorer with a great work ethic and hit the net with regularity. As a captain he was an inspiration. Ross Cook was a rare talent and could surely have played at a must higher level with his ability. The term 'flawed genius' is sometimes used to describe players. They could and should have succeeded but something held them back; Robin Friday at Reading would have been a good example. Cook was a natural goal scorer had skill and pace in abundance which would frighten any defence. Of course he was always going to get rough treatment from defenders and unfortunately Cook did not take kindly to some of the outrageous challenges he received. He often reacted and this led to a plethora of yellow and red cards. Hence opposing teams would target him and deliberately provoke a reaction with the intention of him being sent off. The 2015-16 team won the Combined League by a proverbial mile. A 2-0 win at Westfield secured the title with Steven Duff and Ross Cook the scorers. However, the Green Lane ground was deemed not to be suitable for the Southern League. Chairman

Luke Mullen and his committee apologised and pledged to have the standard improved by the end of the forthcoming season.

The team management and players accepted the situation and virtually all re-signed for the following season, 2016-17. It turned out to be a repeat performance with Hartley Wintney winning the league again in a canter. Sam Argent proved once again to be an inspirational captain. His work ethic was infectious to the other players and his goal-scoring prowess probably second to none. In defence was the experienced Steve Noakes, another inspiring player for the club. This time with a huge effort from the Club Officials the ground improvements were completed on time and Hartley Wintney were duly promoted. This did not go unnoticed down the road at Basingstoke Town. A village club nearby had moved up the pecking order and they were now just one league apart. Clearly there was now competition for the local bragging rights. The gates at the Row were now between 100 to 200 on a regular basis.

Hartley Wintney had moved into the Southern League Division 1 and made a good start. Ross Cook had moved on but Paul Hodges had joined from Abbey Rangers. When covering matches between Abbey Rangers and Hartley Wintney I had rated Hodges the best player in the Division. His signing for the Row was a real bonus. Then local football excitement was aroused within a short time of the season starting. In the FA Cup Basingstoke Town had drawn Hartley Wintney at home. In the matches immediately before the FA Cup match Basingstoke had won 8-0 at Gosport Borough. By contrast The Row had a dreadful afternoon at Marlow in losing 0-3.

In times past this would have been a foregone conclusion and a Basingstoke win virtually assured. Around five years previously the 'Stoke had won an FA Cup match 4-0 at the Camrose. The match would pitch managers Terry Brown and Jason Bristow of Basingstoke against Dan Brownlie and Anthony Millerick for the Row.

Prior to the match Graham Merry of the Gazette and I made our predictions and both of us came up with the same result a 2-2 draw. If a replay Graham predicted a Basingstoke win while I thought Hartley would win by a few goals to spare at Hartley Wintney. I could not see Basingstoke cope with Argent and Hodges. In the first match it looked like our predictions had gone out the window. With 10 minutes to go the 'Stoke led 2-0 and were seemingly on their way to the next round. However, a brace from the sharp Paul Hodges delighted the Row support and it was a 2-2 draw; exactly as predicted. A crowd of around 550 were at the match. A bigger crowd was at Green Lane for the replay with well over 600 present to see a very tight and tense match. In the end a Sam Argent penalty separated the sides to secure a memorable win for the villagers amid much excitement. Basingstoke Town followers were stunned. How on earth could they have lost to a local village team? It did not take them long to respond. Within a few weeks they had put in an approach for the Row Talisman Sam Argent. It was said to be an offer Sam could not refuse. Terry Brown was delighted to have captured such a talented player. Some of his comments irked the Hartley faithful which was only natural. They had parted with someone who was close to their hearts.

However, the management skills of Anthony Millerick and Dan Brownlie came to the fore. They readjusted their style of play. Jake Baxter arrived as a striker; not a Sam Argent but full of running. However, three experienced players were to make a considerable difference and ultimately help the Row to success. Nick Ciardini arrived from Farnborough and after a slow start proved to be very effective. However, the initial replacement for Sam Argent was former Portsmouth, QPR and Birmingham footballer Rowan Vine. If this was to be Vine's swansong towards the end of his career it was a resounding success. He came in at exactly the right moment and lifted morale at the club enormously. The one constant throughout the season was Paul Hodges. 'Hodgie' was a real character. After the matches in the clubhouse he would usually say to me, knowing I did the match reports, 'Did you realise that these two goals I scored today were my 22nd and 23rd of the season?' He was also a decent singer, which appeared on a few YouTube clips.

The season drifted on and Hartley had moved into the playoff places, which was astonishing. They confirmed their place with a match to spare and were drawn at home to AFC Dunstable in the Semi-Final. Row played well and helped mainly by a resolute defence with the dependable Liam Eagle dominant at the back won 2-0. Dean Stow scored from one of his special free kicks and Nick Ciardini took advantage of a defensive slip to secure the win.

The Final was again at home against Cambridge City. A large crowd of over 700 gathered and saw another very tight match with few chances in sweltering heat. The match was decided when A Dean Stow free kick was headed across goal by Jack Ball for Nick Ciardini to score at the back post. Great celebrations followed. Hartley Wintney were now amazingly in the Southern League Premier Division. If the previous seasons had shown the prowess of the forwards as being instrumental in gaining promotion, Season 2017-2018 was different. The defence, including Jack Ball, Steve Noakes, stalwart Liam Eagle, youngster Louie Paget and Dean Stow, provided the bedrock for the team.

Sam Argent proved a great favourite at Basingstoke Town as expected and had a decent scoring record. However, his season was cut short following a bad facial injury.

A mention must be given to the Row goalkeepers who all performed amazingly over the seasons. Craig Atkinson, Paul Strudley, Adam Desbois and Luke Williams.

HARTLEY Wintney maintained their 13-point lead at the top of the Combined Counties Premier League, after an excellent 7-0 victory against an in-form and high-scoring visiting North Greenford United side.

The home side started brightly and took the lead on seven minutes. Dean Stow made a good run down the right wing and his cross found Sam Argent, who smashed the ball into the net.

Hartley opened the second half

Steven Duff scored a superb goal

visitors as they scored four goals in a seven-minute spell.

In the 47th minute a Steven Duff corner was cleared back out to the winger. His inswinging cross was misjudged by the goalkeeper, who could only palm the ball into the net.

Two minutes later, clever hold-up play by Argent saw him feed a well-timed pass into the path of Ross Cook who ran on and scored easily.

In another two minutes it was 4-0, Luke Perkins sending in a

goal from the edge of the box.

On 54 minutes Hartley added a fifth. Perkins' long pass found Cook and he chipped the goalie.

Just after the hour, goal number number six arrived, as a long free-kick from Liam Eagle set up a powerful header from Steve Noakes. This produced an excellent stop by Harry, but Argent netted the rebound.

Eight minutes from time, midfielder Steve Laidler fed Argent who set Cook free for his hat-trick.

Sharpshooting duo hit 148 goals in 16 months

By David Graham
sportsdesk@basingstokegazette.co.uk

MEETING Mr Argent and Mr Cook is an invitation which all defenders in teams in the Combined Counties League Premier Division would gladly decline.

Sam Argent and Ross Cook score goals and they score lots of them.

In the last 16 months the twin strikers of Hartley Wintney have banged in an amazing total of 148 goals. Argent with 77 and Cook 71.

The exploits have helped Hartley to the top of national league goals scored with total of 70 league goals.

This is higher than any team in England, from the top of the Premiership right down to Non League Level Five. If cup matches are counted the Hartley total rises to 90 goals.

The two boys from Oakridge have known one another for some time, although their routes to Green Lane at Hartley came from different directions in the form of the two South coast rivals.

Cook learned his trade courtesy of Portsmouth and Argent with Southampton.

Cook said: "When we met up at the start of the 2015/16 season, we immediately gelled as strikers and it was evident early on that we would have some success."

By the end of the season the pair had netted a remarkable 92 goals between them (Argent 51 and Cook 41).

The goals scored helped Hartley to the Combined Counties Premier League title, as well as excellent runs in the FA Cup and FA Vase.

This season the pair has carried on where they have left

off. In just three months the pair have scored 56 goals between them Cook (30) and Argent (26).

The goals have driven the Row to a large lead at the top of the league again and in addition they knocked out Hampshire Senior Cup holders Havant.

Argent said: "It is a team game and our quest for goals is greatly helped by playing in a team of smashing players.

"We are a close knit unit and we work hard at training with our managers and coaching staff. Dan Brownlie, Anthony Millerick and Luke Tuffs always motivate and prepare us well for every match."

Skipper Sam Argent leads from the front. His selection as team captain was an inspirational choice as he provides a high work rate ethic as an example to the rest of his team.

Ross Cook's total may have been higher had he not been side lined at various parts of the season. Cook said: "I believe in playing with a bit of passion."

The referee's would not argue with this, but probably think he plays with too much passion resulting in yellow and red cards.

This season has seen a vast improvement, despite the fact that he is often the victim of some terrible challenges.

In fact, Hartley are near the top of the division's fair play league for teams with the fewest yellow and red cards.

Hartley's quest for a run in the FA Vase starts with a tough home match against Melksham Town on Saturday.

Both players are looking forward to this.

Argent said: "Last season we played Hereford at home in front of an all-ticket sell out crowd. Although we lost we would like more occasions like this."

Hartley Wintney's deadly duo Ross Cook (left) and Sam Argent

For Hartley Wintney FC they have proven that providing a good match day experience brings success. Luke and Elayne Mullen go out their way to make people feel welcome. Kevin O'Byrne the former Basingstoke Town Director is ace when it comes to Social Media.

One of the best programmes you can find anywhere is produced. An excellent website gives all the latest news at the club. The Clubhouse is kept spotless by a hard-working committee which includes many female members. Add the feeling of a village togetherness and everyone pulling in the same direction gives a good spirit at the club.

For my part I greatly enjoy doing the match reports for the club. Basingstoke Town could do with trying to engender the same sort of togetherness once they see the back of Mr Razzak.

The following 2018-19 season was to show that the Row could mix it well in the higher Southern League Premier. Amazingly they were to play Basingstoke Town four times in this one season. In the League matches the honours were shared. Hartley won 3-1 at the Camrose with goals from Romario Hart, Ross Cook and Louie Paget. The game at Hartley Wintney saw a good performance from Basingstoke who deservedly won 2-0. Sam Smart was the man of the match and scored a spectacular goal. The other two fixtures saw Basingstoke win 3-1 at Hartley in the Hampshire Cup. However the Row evened things up with a 4-1 win in the Evo-Stik Cup with Sal Abubakar netting a brace.

During match days we have a little team to help with the media coverage. Tyler House does the Twitter and Josie Shipman provides the match photos. In a season it is amazing how many goals Josie manages to catch with amazing concentration. Kevin O'Byrne does the website and is a very influential member of the club. During match days I try to keep up with who scored the goal as well as who took the corner or made the pass etc. I have some good helpers in Mike, Tony, Ray and many others. Their concentration levels are far better than mine. I enjoy the company of the referees' assessors who certainly are eagle eyed. If they award a penalty to the Row I tell them to put down a tick on their sheet!! The current shutdown at time of writing I greatly miss watching the club play.

With match reporting I send the copies to a number of newspapers. I am fortunate that I get quotes from the managers. Dan Brownlie was always good and concise before he moved to Basingstoke Town. Anthony Millerick (Millers) always offers to provide comments for a match report. Over the years I have seen many football managers. Alex Ferguson of course operates at a much higher level. When watching Slough Town they had Bob Gibbs, the local headmaster at Slough Grammar School who paved the way for much success. He was replaced by Tommy Lawrence, a former Enfield manager who took them to a new level. At Basingstoke Town I thought Trevor Parker was good but he left after just one season after a dispute of some sort. Jason Bristow did well and will be even better with his new experiences at Eastleigh. However, I rate Anthony Millerick highly. He knows what he wants and how to achieve it. Always a good quality in a manager. In addition he is open and communicates easily with the entire club.

TYLER HOUSE (MEDIA TEAM), JACK BALL
AND ANTHONY MILLERICK IN BACKGROUND
TOP PHOTO BY PAUL PAXFORD,
PHOTO ABOVE BY JOSIE SHIPMAN

CHAPTER 20

THE COUNCIL FROM HELL

 Basingstoke and Deane Borough Council in the years 2017 and 2018 were making a name for themselves. However, it was not in a positive fashion. It revolved around high Executive Officer salaries and a complete lack of any form of transparency.

The Executive Officers in any Council are important people and should be held accountable to the elected Councillors. Also they should be able to answer questions on who they appoint to key positions. Up till the Camrose Scandal came along I took little or no interest in the functionality of how the Council worked. The wrong assumption I made was that the senior non-elected officers had the day-to-day functions to take care of in their relative spheres of duties. They would be answerable to the Council Chamber if something untoward cropped up. The Councillors on the other hand would take up issues on the constituents' behalf and feedback would be provided. Nothing could be further from the truth from my experiences and observations since 2017.

In my opinion the Basingstoke and Deane Executive has too much power. My suspicion is that they are there to carry out the wishes of Central Government with people in key positions. A main issue in Basingstoke is housing. Without doubt most would recognise that most towns need more houses as the population increases. However, this brings in the questions on where the houses should be built. In my opinion a Football Ground should not be given up lightly and if it has to be given up then a replacement must be built.

The Planning and Finance of Building Developments must be tightly controlled and seen to be totally above board with integrity paramount. The Basingstoke Golf Club Development led to the exposure of Andrew Finney, a senior Councillor. Finney is a Non-Executive Director of Centerprise, the company owned by Rafi Razzak. He was forced to apologise to the Council when it emerged his wife was a member of the Golf Club and in line for a large pay-out when the Developers got their approval. He had previously been voting in the Council Chambers on the Golf Club Development project. Finney has since given up being a Councillor. However, his link to Rafi Razzak was brought to the fore when the abortive attempt was made to get approval for the Down Grange Proposal.

From reading information in the public domain it is obvious that the Councillors are not always given the full facts on all the issues. This was never more apparent than with the Camrose Scandal. The complete acceptance that a Covenant should be given up because it is 'lost' was truly absurd to virtually everyone. One would have expected the Basingstoke Executive to review the situation and make sure they produced a report to say that the Camrose Covenant must be preserved. However, the recent history of this Executive shows that this would be wishful thinking.

An article in the Inside Croydon appeared during 2018.

THE GODFATHER: GRAHAM CADLE

Croydon Council's Godfather has found himself a new job.

Graham Cadle, the sometime assistant chief exec at Fisher's Folly, left Croydon Council at the start of the year apparently tired of being reminded that the crap app (© Inside Croydon) which he'd commissioned from Harwinder "Harry" Singh still failed to work properly, despite his throwing millions of public money at it.

Cadle had even hired Singh on £787 per day to work on the council's IT projects, but forgot to volunteer the information to the council management that he was godfather to the child Singh and Karen Sullivan, the council's head of revenues and benefits, had had together.

Cadle, Singh and Sullivan have ended their work at Croydon Council, following a second formal investigation into their conduct, arising from an Inside Croydon investigation last year. Though Jo Negrini, the council chief executive, has refused to answer any questions about the value of the pay-offs which may have been made to senior staffers Cadle and Sullivan.

Cadle was one of the council's top-paid executives before his departure.

Now, Inside Croydon understands that he has been appointed to a "highly paid post" by Basingstoke and Deane Borough Council in Hampshire, where he is to take up the position of interim head of finance and resources.

Cadle's predecessor there was Kevin Jaquest, who was paid around £115,000 a year, according to official figures.

Jaquest was at the centre of a data breach row earlier this year, when Basingstoke was reported to the Information Commissioner over complaints about its handling of personal information.

Basingstoke council's press office refused to outline the circumstances of long-serving Jaquest's departure from the authority, though they did say it was not connected "in any way" to the data breach.

Which might come as something of a relief to residents and councillors there as they await Cadle's arrival. It was Cadle, after all, who when at Croydon managed the "digital enabling" project which burned through a £8.2 million annual budget in just five months.

And it was Cadle who authorised Singh to off-shore elements of Croydon Council's data management project to India, potentially "opening the back door" to the council computer system and putting tens of thousands of confidential records at risk – and going against ICO recommendations.

This revelation led to a look into the performance of Kevin Jaquest at Basingstoke Council. It did not make pretty reading!! The first search found that a number of staff were a very unhappy bunch, never a good sign especially in a Council.

Article from the Basingstoke Gazette in December 2017:

MORE staff have left a council department in which there has been accusations of psychological bullying.

Multiple sources have reported two further staff members have resigned from posts while part of Basingstoke and Deane Borough Council's (BDBC) law and governance unit, one of whom was a senior employee.

The Gazette is not naming the senior employee but they are understood to be highly respected in their field.

BDBC executive director of finance and resources Kevin Jaquest said: "It would not be appropriate for us to discuss specific staffing matters publicly, especially to give information on individuals or to respond to speculative comments.

"The day-to-day operation of the council in its role as an employer is dealt with appropriately by management and regularly reported to councillors through the HR Committee."

Last month, The Gazette reported a former member of staff within the unit said absence due to stress and anxiety are at 'epidemic levels' and that within the roughly 40 person-strong law and governance unit, ten people left between June 2016 and September 2017, nine by resigning.

A Freedom of Information (FoI) request showed staff absence to stress, depression and other mental health problems in the unit stood at 566 days between June 2016 and September 2017 – nearly 80 per cent of overall absence.

In the year 2016/17 sickness leave due to stress or anxiety across the council was around 28 per cent of total staff absence.

The staff member alleged psychological bullying within the department led to the high levels of absence due to stress and anxiety.

Other sources have told The Gazette spending on locum staff within the unit has risen while up until Monday, BDBC was also advertising for two principal lawyer posts which offered a 10 per cent of starting salary – of £46,654 – Introductory payment to attract staff to the authority.

This article reveals a culture of bullying the staff. However, worse than that was revealed when it became apparent that the Basingstoke and Deane Borough Council Executive could withhold information from the Councillors without giving a good reason. This Gazette article in February 2018 raised a few eyebrows.

A 'SERIOUS' breach of data protection has taken place at the borough council with councillors unable to discuss the matter on legal advice.

A document about the breach being reported to the Information Commissioner's Office (ICO) was presented to councillors at a Basingstoke and Deane Borough Council meeting on Monday last week.

However, the audit and accounts committee was told by Kevin Jaquest, the borough council's executive director of finance and resources, it would be 'inappropriate' for the issue to be discussed.

After repeated attempts to ask questions from councillors, Mr Jacquest added: "We have had strong legal advice and as the paper says it's a part of our process which is of notifying of the referral. It is not appropriate at this stage for members to discuss it and the report is very clear that it is a report for noting."

At the meeting, Lib Dem councillor Keith Watts, who said he had lodged three questions about the matter beforehand, said: "I don't accept that at all. The reputational damage of us not discussing it would be relevant here I would have thought."

Labour councillor David Potter said: "It has gone into the public realm already by being on the agenda. I would not want a discussion, just some questions."

Despite this, further questions were not answered with the chairman of the panel, Cllr Roger Gardiner, drawing a line under the item, but adding it was 'not satisfactory'.

Cllr Potter added: "As far as I am concerned this is unacceptable in the sense that it appears on our agenda, there is a report that gives some information clearly, a significant amount of information in regard to the determination of this matter having been classified as serious, and yet beyond that we're not allowed to make any comment or ask any questions. That really is unacceptable I think."

A serious breach is defined as an incident of 'potential detriment to individuals' or 'sensitivity of the data'.

The breach was reported to the ICO on December 12 last year with the council meeting report detailing potential risks including reputational damage and a fine from the ICO which can impose £500,000 fines for the most serious breaches of the Data Protection Act. It could be several months before the ICO makes a decision on the case.

However, all was well when the Council had appointed Graham Cadle to sort all the problems out at a huge salary. This of course begs the obvious question. 'Was Cadle a unique candidate for this post?' Graham Cadle did not stay long and moved on to a similar position at South Gloucestershire Council.

There was no doubt that Jaquest was well rewarded for his work. An article from one of the local newspapers in 2018:

Executive director of finance and resources, Kevin Jaquest, received £113,906, while the executive director of borough services Rebecca Emmett was paid £112,049.

CHAPTER 21

IT'S ALL LEGAL – PHILLIPS THE SOLICITORS

There can be no doubt that Phillips the Solicitors have been a major help to Rafi Razzak over the past two decades. I cannot blame him for using the Solicitors at Town Gate in the town.

For around 24 years I was the owner of a small engineering business. As an engineer I relied on the professional classes to give me advice from their particular sphere. In the case of getting financial advice I used an advisor called Trevor Ward and we usually met in a pub between Dorking and Guildford. His advice was always sound and he was always a great help. In the case of Accountants I probably used four or five over the years. In general I found that it always seemed to be a case of trying to sort what was Tax deductible and what was not. Our paperwork was impeccable; my ex-wife Sue did the Accounts for 17 years. Every invoice was accounted for and we kept every single receipt. We paid all our suppliers within 30 days with only one or two exceptions. These were on two occasions when a Contractor who owed us a lot of money in relative terms went bust. We asked our suppliers for a month's grace until we got our cash flow going again and we moved on from there. When the Tax people called they were always impressed and we never once had to pay any back Tax. With Accountants I found there was always a bit of bartering; I felt in some cases they were working for the Tax Man. In the case of Solicitors it was always Phillips; first at Wolverton Court and then at Town Gate. I found them to be excellent. Fortunately we did not have to call on their services very often but when we did they were professional.

A gentleman called Howard Gardiner helped with my divorce and another name I remember was Alex Preshaw. Hence no great surprise that Rafi Razzak would be impressed by them. Phillips the Solicitors were sponsors to Basingstoke Town before Razzak got involved with the club. It was under John Phillips at the time who always had an advert in the programme. That is why, I and I imagine many others, started using this professional service. In the late 1990s Rafi Razzak and a partner from Phillips called Jonathan Pender became acquainted and this relationship was to last a long time.

In 2001 the club put faith in Rafi Razzak in his venture to set up a Limited Company. At the time they owed a substantial amount of money to the Inland Revenue and other creditors. They put faith in Rafi Razaak because of his acumen in the business world. The club supporters expected investment and a dynamic set of businesspeople to drive the club forward. Phillips' first act was to set up the paperwork which started with the company being incorporated. Jonathan Pender did the needy and in no time Company Director David Knight was signing things off. The Resolution of Memorandum was then produced.

I am not a legal person hence my reliance on Phillips the Solicitors. However, over the years when I was employed as a Commissioning/Service Manager I was involved with the process of accepting orders for our company's Goods and Services. In over 90% of the cases there was never a problem. Most companies worked to similar sets of industry-standard conditions. However, from time to time a set of Contract conditions would be offered which looked insecure. These would involve conditions like: Payment terms, such as pay when paid; Penalty clauses which would be unfair, and Liability for just about everything that would ever go wrong on a Contract. I always made a point of rejecting those types of conditions. If the client still wanted to use our company then it had to be on our terms.

If someone had offered me the conditions in the Resolution of Memorandum I would have very quickly rejected them. Unfortunately Razzak had no one willing to oppose or survey these conditions. The Basingstoke Town officials trusted Rafi Razzak and also Phillips. The conditions essentially implied to me that he could do what he liked. The references to AGMs may have been a check. However, from the limited information available, those meetings which did take place saw no effective challenge to the owner. In 2006 Basron was formed and Phillips the Solicitors were involved again.

Submissions to Companies House on behalf of Basingstoke Town Ltd throughout almost two decades came from Phillips offices at Town Gate. The annual accounts in my limited opinion were scant. As a small business I doubt we would have been allowed to get away with such submissions.

When people look at Solicitors we think about them in terms of the legal word. We lean on them heavily to guide us through the paperwork involved on a particular issue. However, Solicitors in a dispute are adversarial. It is one Solicitor representing an individual or a body. They sometimes are up against another Solicitor hoping to win through for their client. Because they know the law does not mean they represent the law. Phillips are a private company and make good profits. They are a well-oiled money-making enterprise. If a multi-millionaire offers them a substantial amount of business then it would be surprising if they turned it down. Certainly another Solicitor in Basingstoke would probably step in and take up the offer.

When it comes to making moral judgements I would not have taken the steps Phillips took. We now have a situation where football fans are having to travel to Winchester while the town tries to slug it out with the authorities to get the football ground back. The fans are out of pocket collectively to the tune of £50K a season in travel they would not have needed if they stayed at the Camrose. A number of these fans like myself would have given Phillips business over the years.

It has been said that Phillips managed to get a lease of sorts through a 3rd party in an attempt to attack the Covenant. Hence one part of the debate is how legal it is to do something like that. I would not know. The other contentious issue is who the Covenant was left to. Most were under the impression it was 'To the people of Basingstoke to be used for sporting purposes'. This is clear cut in my opinion. However, apologists for Razzak suggest that the Covenant was left to two officers at the Basingstoke Town football club. As it turns out the two individuals concerned were both Aldermen – Cyril Wood and Frank Spencer Spurling were one and the same. However, I believe it was as Aldermen that they received the Lord Camrose Covenant. The football club has had several changes in guises over the years and it is doubtful whether it is clear whether the Covenant went from one to the other. The current assertion is that the Covenant belongs to the club playing as Basingstoke at the Camrose. Hence Basron own the ground. Razzak owns Basingstoke Town Ltd. However, the Covenant belongs to the club who should be playing at the Camrose which is of course the Basingstoke Town Community Club.

I am not knowledgeable enough to confirm what is legally right or wrong. It can get too complicated and that is where the Solicitors come in. In 2017 when the scandal came to prominence we discussed the issue between us one lunchtime at Barton's Mill. The assertion was that the issues were so complicated that Razzak's take on the Covenant being invalid could not be challenged. This was because the cost would be too great for the Council. Plus, of course, as the Covenant was probably 'lost', the original wording was paramount and had to be seen.

Phillips the Solicitors' name does crop up a lot in respect to the Camrose ground.

- They are the Solicitors to Basingstoke Town FC Ltd.

- They were the Solicitors to Basingstoke Town Football and Social Club Ltd.

- Local Basingstoke Councillor Hayley Eachus is a Solicitor at Phillips.

- Local Basingstoke Councillor and also Hampshire County Councillor Elaine Still is employed at Phillips.

- Basron are one of Phillips' clients.

- Rafi Razzak has a close working relationship with Phillips the Solicitors.

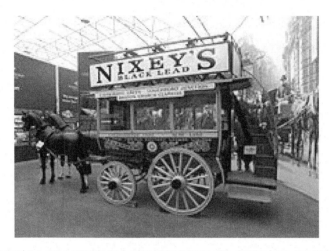

THE MAN ON THE BACK OF THE CLAPHAM OMNIBUS

This took me back to my days as a Commissioning/Service Manager. I remember having a particularly difficult Contract dispute involving all sorts of contractual and technical issues. I felt my counterpart in the opposing firm was lying through his teeth in the dispute. As luck would have it one of our clients who I dealt with was a gentleman called Frank Kelly and he was the Chief Engineer at the Barbican Arts Centre in the City of London. He was the oracle on legal issues involving technical aspects. He thought I was right but could see the difficulty in taking it to any form of judgement. However, his advice was spot on and I used it throughout the rest of my working life. He asked me if I had heard of the 'Man on the Clapham Omnibus' case to which I replied 'no'. In 1903 a Judge in a complicated trial in the high court stopped the trial mid-way through as he could see the jury were bamboozled. He said, 'Look, if you were the man on the back of the Clapham Omnibus how would you judge this? The man sitting at the back of the Clapham Omnibus would have average intelligence. He is of average income and no bias to anyone. What would he say?'

Subsequently it did not take the Jury long to come up with a verdict as they were able to cut through a number of the red herrings which were being thrown in. Hence, if someone was making a judgement on the Lord Camrose Covenant, who would they favour? Would it be the Lord Camrose and the people of Basingstoke? Or alternatively would it be Rafi Razaak and Phillips the Solicitors saying that it had been sorted through some 3rd party leasing company? To an ordinary person like me it is a no-brainer.

On Social Media a letter appeared which seemed to show Phillips the Solicitors and Basron working together to try and dislodge the Lord Camrose Covenant.

DAVID GRAHAM

Mr M McPhail
Basron Developments Limited
Brinkletts House
Winchester Road
Basingstoke
Hampshire RG21 8UE

Our Ref: JRP/SD/Basron Developments Limited/22962-1
Your Ref: MM

24 January 2018

Dear Malcolm

BASINGSTOKE TOWN FOOTBALL CLUB
CAMROSE FOOTBALL GROUND WINCHESTER ROAD BASINGSTOKE HAMPSHIRE

I refer to recent communications in respect of restrictive covenants allegedly binding upon the freehold interest in respect of the above property.

The Council will no doubt be aware that the above land was owned by Lord Camrose/his Trustees and latterly through the 140 Trustee Company Limited for many years.

Attached is a copy of freehold title HP609233 as possessed by the 140 Trustee Company Limited and this land has now been acquired by Basron Developments Limited the current registered proprietor.

The title reveals no restrictive covenants. These would show in the Charges Register. There is no reference whatsoever to any covenants.

The Council will also be aware that in order to procure registered title the Land Registry would require disclosure of all unregistered title deeds and documents. As part of the process of First Registration, which was undertaken by Camrose Estate/Trust, is the Land Registry's statutory obligation to carry across all matters which affect the property onto the title registers at the time of First Registration.

It can be seen that the Land Registry determined that no restrictive covenants existed or were considered either relevant or binding or that it was appropriate that they be registered.

The acquisition by Basron Developments Limited was of the land on this title and a copy of its title entries are also attached.

Phillips Solicitors Town Gate 88 London Street Basingstoke Hampshire RG21 7NY
01256 460830   01256 854898   legal@phillips-law.co.uk   phillips-law.co.uk   129079 Basingstoke 10

142

The issue of alleged freehold restrictive covenants binding the property cannot legally be supported and is not correct.

Yours sincerely

Jonathan Pender
PHILLIPS
email: jonathan.pender@phillips-law.co.uk
Direct Dial: 01256 854613
Fax: +44 (0) 1256 854638

Encl.

Title Entries HP609233 (The 140 Trust Company Limited)
Title Entries HP609233 (The Basron Developments Limited)

Phillips Solicitors Town Gate 36 London Street Basingstoke Hampshire RG21 7NY
01256 460830   01256 854633   legal@phillips-law.co.uk   phillips-law.co.uk   128079 Basingstoke 10

CHAPTER 22

TO WINCHESTER WE GO

The move to Winchester City was hard to take for the football fraternity in Basingstoke. An aspect to it was the considerable time lag in setting up some sorts of deals with the Collaboration. Talks with the Hampshire Football Association were proving difficult with complications. The HFA were allocated – separately from the club – money from the Football Foundation to install a 3G pitch at their headquarters at Winklebury. In addition some additional work was carried out in the surrounds. Separate from that there was some other work to be done for the Basingstoke Town Community Club. Also Basingstoke Town Community Club were given the green light for part mitigation for the move to Winklebury from the Football Foundation.

Prior to all that there was to be a transfer of the Lease from Basingstoke Council to the HFA in order that they could work in Collaboration with the Community Club. In the opinion of many including myself this was all a complete waste of time. The core issue was that no statement was made on how the Camrose ground was going to be replaced. It appeared that Basingstoke Council and the Community Club were willing to accept £250K to install an enhancement at Winklebury. In exchange the town were to give up a ground on land valued at around £5 to £6 million for housing development. It meant the loss of one of the town's two main football arenas. Not a good deal!!

The Basingstoke Town relegation saw an exodus of virtually their entire playing squad. Manager Martin Kuhl was effectively starting again and had to recruit quickly. To the end of their time at the Camrose it is understood the Community Club were not afforded any of the income from the Camrose Clubhouse. Also they did not receive gate money and were obliged to pay the players' wages. In other words, a pretty rotten deal. At Winchester they were able to collect gate money but did not receive any of the income from the bar takings. They went to Winchester City. The season started badly with a home defeat against Barnstable by 4-3 and things did not get much better throughout a torrid season. Before the Covid-19 lockdown they stood second bottom of the Division with only Barnstable below them. Fortunately in this Division only one team was to be relegated instead of the usual three. There were three pretty bruising 8-0 defeats for the supporters to endure. Martin Kuhl departed and was replaced with the former Hartley Wintney co manager Dan Brownlie. Of course he was on a 'Mission Impossible' and despite trying to change things by bringing in new players the team unit did not gel.

The Community Club put in a huge effort to achieve getting to

Winklebury. Winklebury was a 'mitigation' for a loss. However, the real 'mitigation' was the replacement of the Camrose. At no stage did the Community Club make any effort to challenge and try and get the Camrose replaced. Councillor Simon Bounds also moved along the same track with never a word on how the Camrose was to be replaced. It is difficult to believe both the Community Club and Councillor Bounds thought this was a sensible option as a replacement. However, one man who would have thought it was a fantastic deal was Rafi Razzak.

A few Community Club meetings were held at the Apollo Hotel but nothing of substance could be offered as to the way forward.

The Camrose ground soon went to the derelict stage and the owner sold off goal posts and the dugout shelters. From the outside it looked like a dump and a very poor advertisement for Basingstoke. Most but not all towns and villages take a pride in their football stadiums. Being a modern town Basingstoke were offering up a dump. A ground deliberately degraded by its owner. The only motive appeared to be just pure greed.

A good summary of the Winklebury situation is provided by respected Basingstoke football writer Ken Gaunt. Clearly the promised £250,000 was not going to stretch too far. Once again no budgets and no proper planning.

£750,000 needed for ground works at new Basingstoke Town home.

Aug 13, 2019 | Chimp Weekly Headlines, Headlines, Newsnow

By Ken Gaunt

Basingstoke Town owner Rafi Razzak has been told £750,000 is needed for ground works at the community club's new Winklebury home.

That is £500,000 more than Razzak pledged but only, he maintains, when planning permission for 89 homes at the Camrose is approved.

He did not baulk at the new figure, according to community club director Kevin White, who had a three-hour meeting with the owner, along with coach Dan Brownlie.

Razzak is also a director of Basron, the company that own the site, and well-connected Basingstoke businessman White said: "It was the most positive meeting we have had so far.

"They share our interest in getting into Winklebury as soon as possible, which is good. The final figures we said would be needed for the renovations would be around three quarters of a million pounds, which we are trying to negotiate.

"They are saying the value is in getting planning permission on the Camrose. There would be little money from them until that happened with potentially a further payment when the Camrose is sold.

"What they have not done is worked out: what are the costs to buy (the land)? what are the anticipated playing costs? what are the anticipated legal costs? what is the cost of the club rehousing? And what is the end product?

"What I am doing is putting all this into a legal contract. We need to thrash a few of the details out in fairness."

Basingstoke, who were relegated to the Southern League South division on the last day of the season, start their campaign against Barnstaple at home on Saturday at Winchester.

Martin Kuhl's side are sharing with their league rivals before moving to Winklebury, where the community club are working in partnership with the Hampshire FA, who are based there.

White said: "We want the C ground grading at Winklebury We do not want to go into something that is inferior.

"If you are handing over this club to a community club, it should be a changing of the guard, not running it into the ground, which is what it seems.

"The dugouts have been sold, the goalposts and training goals have been sold, so have four of the five turnstiles. What annoyed me was we wanted first refusal."

White added: "We gave them the figures we want, they did not say no. Hopefully we can get through negotiations.

"With staged payments made, planning permission and final sale we get to that three quarters of a million, which we need for the clubhouse and all the other things.

"I use an analogy with the current owners, if my parents lived in the house I owned and I wanted to develop the house and sell up, part of the cost of that development is the re-housing costs of my parents.

"So what am I going to buy for them to live in? Stamp duty, the legal fees, you take all that off and you have some profit at the end."

Away from the Winchester fiasco we were making some progress in trying to get the Camrose ground back on the agenda. Somehow there appeared to be a misunderstanding between what was meant as a 'Replacement' as opposed to a 'Mitigation'.

CHAPTER 23

THE PLANNING APPLICATION GOES IN

CAMROSE TOWN END – STOKIE WATCHES FROM THE
TERRACE

In April 2019 the long awaited Planning Application went in. I had
been waiting for it, of course, with others. I thought that I should get
myself prepared. The first thing was to find out how to find out
information on what was going on from the Basingstoke Council
website. After some time trying I finally fathomed out how to
monitor what was happening with Planning Applications. This

website is not easy to navigate and is user vicious. However, the Planning Application for the Houses was:

Outline application for the erection of up to 89 dwellings with associated access and external works, following the demolition of the existing Basingstoke Town FC stand and terraces (all matters reserved except access)

After a few weeks I started to check what objections and comments had been received. First to show was the Portfolio holder Councillor Simon Bounds' submission. I found it jaw dropping!!

From: Cllr Simon Bound Sent: 30 May 2019 20:59 To: PlanningComments Cc: Subject: 19/01110/OUT | Outline application for the erection of up to 89 dwellings with associated access

After keeping a close eye on the development of this application, attending meetings with the football club fans and meetings with Hants FA & the community club I have some concerns that are directly related to this application. These concerns relate directly to the commitments made by the owners of the ground and the football club regarding the move of the football club to the Winklebury football complex and the ground improvements that are required. The loss of the Camrose site is difficult for fans and the town to accept but the ground and club are currently privately owned and it appears they can therefore do what they want. In the conversations and meetings around the development of the site commitments have been made by the owners, and their representatives, to providing significant financial support. This financial support has been stated as £250,000 for ground improvements at Winklebury and in addition putting the football club in a debt free position so the Football Association license can be transferred to the community club's ownership. In the most recent meetings some doubt has now been expressed about the amount and timing of investment by the owners into the Winklebury site. This investment in the Winklebury site by the club/site owners is essential for a successful move. I would ask for the planning authority to do everything in its power to hold the owners to the investment that is required to deliver a successful move to Winklebury for the club. I would also like to reserve my right to speak at the Development Control Committee. Simon Bound Deputy Leader Member for Rooksdown

It confirmed that for whatever reason the Council had given up on finding the Covenant that had been given to the Council. They just accepted that Rafi Razzak was the Leaseholder, being the owner of Basingstoke Town FC Ltd. In addition it confirmed that the Council were willing to accept a £250K enhancement to the HFA headquarters at Winklebury in exchange for giving away the Camrose ground to Basron.

Three other Councillors quickly were to put in objections to the Proposals. These were Sean Keating, Gary Watts and Colin Regan who were the Councillors for the Wards adjacent to the Camrose. Neighbourhood comments quickly followed, all opposed to the Basron Development.

The one comment I was watching for was the one from Sport England. This was to prove decisive in my opinion. It certainly was comprehensive in every single way!! 89% of recommendations made by Sport England to Councils in the South East of England are accepted. The 11% who do not accept soon find their sports provision diminishes. It is a lengthy submission and conclusive.

Dear Trevor,

Thank you for consulting Sport England on the above outline application for the erection of up to 89 dwellings with associated access and external works, and the demolition of the existing Basingstoke Town FC stand and terraces (all matters reserved except access) Sport England – Statutory Role and Policy.

It is understood that the proposal prejudices the use, or leads to the loss of use, of land being used as a playing field or has been used as a playing field in the last five years, as defined in the Town and Country Planning (Development Management Procedure) (England) Order 2015 (Statutory Instrument 2015 No. 595). The consultation with Sport England is therefore a statutory requirement. Sport England has considered the application in light of the National Planning Policy Framework (particularly Para 97) and Sport England's Playing Fields Policy, which is presented within its 'Playing Fields Policy and Guidance Document':

www.sportengland.org/playingfieldspolicy.

Sport England's policy is to oppose the granting of planning permission for any development which would lead to the loss of, or prejudice the use of, all/part of a playing field, unless one or more of the five exceptions stated in its policy apply.

The Proposal and Impact on Playing Field

The proposed development will result in the entire loss of playing field at the site which comprises the adult stadia pitch used by Basingstoke FC; the associated ancillary facilities; as well as the two small-sided 3G artificial grass training pitches/MUGAs to the north east of the main stadia pitch. Sport England notes that the applicant asserts in their planning statement that the proposal meets Policy CN8 within Basingstoke and Deane's Local Plan, specifically in relation to parts (e) and (f) and in part (g). Policy CN8 states: Proposals that would result in the loss of valued facilities currently or last used for the provision of community, leisure and cultural activities will only be permitted if it is demonstrated that: e) The facility is no longer needed for any of the functions that it can perform; or f) It is demonstrated that it is no longer practical, desirable or viable to retain them; or g) Any proposed replacement or improved facilities will be equivalent or better in terms of quality, quantity and accessibility and there will be no overall reduction in the level of facilities in the area in which the existing development is located; or 2 h) The proposal will clearly provide sufficient community benefit to outweigh the loss of the existing facility, meeting evidence of a local need. The applicant argues that parts e) and f) of the policy are met as the football club can no longer perform essential functions; and it is no longer practical; viable or desirable for its current use. The applicant goes on to argue that part g) is met in part as well as a result of securing enhancements to the stadium pitch at Winklebury. Sport England has consulted the Football Foundation (FF) on behalf of the FA (the national governing body for football) and has received the following comments.

The Football Foundation comments that they dispute the agent's assertion in para 6.18 of the planning statement that Basingstoke Town Community Football Club (BTCFC) desired a move away from the Camrose Stadium or that the site was no longer needed. The club had no option on this matter. The FF further dispute the argument that the deterioration in quality of the facility is also used as a reason for disposal. However, the FF contends that this is down to lack of investment due to longer term plans to sell the site for development. The FF confirms that the site is still the home ground for a Step 3 level club and the 5-aside artificial pitches are still in regular use. The Football Foundation go on to comment that Basron as landowners of the Camrose Stadium facilities have not contributed to the development of the 3rd generation (3G) rubber crumb artificial grass pitch (AGP) at Winklebury. The 3G stadia pitch has been already identified as a priority project in the last Playing Pitch Strategy and has been funded through the Football Foundation, Hampshire FA and Basingstoke and Deane Council. Community usage had already been agreed with local clubs such as Winklebury Wizards FC, Basingstoke Town Ladies FC and Chineham FC and this project would have progressed without the involvement of BTCFC. The FF comment that a number of adjustments have been made to accommodate BTCFC or otherwise risk them going out of business due to a lack of facility.

The Winklebury Complex was identified as a project that was needed in addition to the Camrose as highlighted in the original application to the Foundation for the grass stadia pitch back in 2003. At the time of the last Playing Pitch Strategy plans for the Camrose were unknown, and the Winklebury development was not identified as a replacement project. The FF note that as the current Winklebury ground is designed to meet Step 6 requirements, as a minimum the ancillary facilities need to be upgraded to Step 3 in order to provide equivalent facilities to those being lost at Camrose. This should include stands, turnstiles and a clubhouse and will form part of an imminent planning application from BTCFC. Planning and funding for the 3G element of this project has already been approved with works due to start in June 2019 and completion in August 2019. In order to allow future development of the site then a certain amount of hard standing is required to allow for stands to be fitted retrospectively as the timing of this planning application, and the one from BTCFC, has not aligned with the timescales for the 3G. BTCFC are having to provide the cost of these works at £53,815 but this cost should also have been part of any mitigation strategy. The FF further comment that if the 3G artificial training pitches are lost at Camrose, the number and the frequency of use of academy and youth team teams cannot be accommodated at Winklebury, as Basingstoke Town Community Club has already used plenty of slots and the remainder need to be available for wider community use. The pitches are also well used by local junior clubs who equally cannot be accommodated at Winklebury because of other demand.

Therefore, without suitable mitigation for loss of these facilities being identified to replace the training pitches (or pitch), some additional funding should be made available to potentially enhance the informal MUGA at Winklebury Playing Fields for wider community benefit as part of the regeneration of the Winklebury area and this should be a compliant smallsided 3G facility. The FF notes that because of the beneficial arrangement linking the relocation of BTCFC with the already planned facility at Winklebury, the costs have been greatly reduced in comparison with securing equivalent replacement provision on a new site. The FF considers that it is only reasonable to expect the costs of the ancillary facilities needed to bring the ground up to Step Level 3 requirements and secure compensation for the loss of training pitch facilities to be provided as a mitigation for that which is being lost. The FF would ask what mitigation is being proposed to mitigate the loss of the grass pitch at Camrose?

3 Therefore the FF objects to this application until a Section 106 agreement is provided to meet the requirements outlined above. It is important to recognise that the development of a 3G community facility at Winklebury was being developed irrespective of the future of the Camrose Site. Assessment against Sport England Policy/NPPF Sport England notes the comments from the FF on behalf of the FA above. Sport England notes that while the Council's Playing Pitch Strategy (PPS) did identify that there was a sufficient supply of adult pitches to meet current and future demand, it also identified that there was an insufficient supply of grass pitches for youth and mini soccer. The PPS recommended that use of the existing provision and provision of new pitches needed to be managed flexibly to cater for changes in demand. The PPS went on to identify a shortfall in 3G pitch provision especially to meet current and future demand for mini-soccer and youth football. It identified an action to support the Hants FA to secure funding to provide an Artificial Grass Pitch with community use to replace the grass pitch as the main stadium pitch at Winklebury. Sport England contends that there is no indication within the PPS that the development of the 3G pitch at Winklebury is identified as replacement provision for that being lost at Camrose. Further, there is no suggestion within the PPS that the pitch and facilities at Camrose are surplus to requirements and that there is an excess of playing field within the catchment which justifies the loss of playing field/pitches and associated facilities. It should be noted that the development of the 3G stadia pitch at Winklebury will result in the loss of an existing adult grass pitch under the permission ref: 18/01309/FUL. This proposal would see a further loss of an adult grass pitch in the borough which is not justified as evidenced by the Council's PPS.

Sport England agrees with the Football Foundation that there is insufficient mitigation proposed for the loss of ancillary facilities and artificial grass training pitches at the Camrose Stadium site and that upgraded and improved facilities are required at Winklebury to bring the new 3G stadia pitch facility upto the required level. Sport England considers that the applicant should be required to mitigate the loss of existing facilities and enter into a Section 106 agreement to provide financial contributions towards equivalent ancillary provision including turnstiles; grandstands; and improvements to existing stands and a new clubhouse required at Winklebury to bring the ground upto Step 3 level requirements as well as equivalent training pitch facilities. Conclusion In light of the above, Sport England objects to the application because it is not considered to accord with any of the exceptions to Sport England's Playing Fields Policy or with Paragraph 97 of the NPPF. Sport England considers that a mitigation package addressing the elements above as part of a Section 106 agreement is required in order to broadly meet our E4 policy and para 97 of the NPPF.

Our E4 exception policy states: 'The area of playing field to be lost as a result of the proposed development will be replaced, prior to the commencement of development, by a new area of playing field:

• of equivalent or better quality, and

• of equivalent or greater quantity, and

• in a suitable location, and

• subject to equivalent or better accessibility and management arrangements.'

We would be happy to work with the local authority and the applicant to discuss and agree the contents of a Section 106 agreement to ensure that suitable mitigation is delivered within a satisfactory timescale. If this application is to be presented to a Planning Committee, we would like to be notified in advance of the publication of any committee agendas, report(s) and committee date(s). We would be grateful if you would advise us of the outcome of the application by sending us a copy of the decision notice. If you would like any further information or advice please contact me at the address below

Yours sincerely,

Owen Neal (MRTPI) Planning Manager

The comments from Sport England and the Football Foundation were scathing towards Rafi Razzak and his Basron company. Sport England are a much respected statutory body and had clearly seen through the motives of the developer. Astonishingly Basingstoke Council and the Basingstoke Town Community Club did not pick up on the recommendations. They still pursued the line of getting the £250K enhancement to Winklebury money from Rafi Razzak.

It was also becoming very apparent that Basron may not have

actually gained the Covenant as most had assumed. It was very unclear and threw up a considerable number of questions.

a) When Basingstoke Town FC Ltd was set up in 2002 there was a 34-page document produced. There was not one mention of the Covenant being transferred. It was 'assumed' that it naturally belonged to Razzak and his Limited Company. However, the previous Basingstoke Town Football and Social Club did not stop trading until 2005!!

b) A Preferential Share worth £5,000 was supposed to ensure that the fans had representation on the Limited Company. This was to ensure no one person could take over the company and act against the best interests of the football club.

c) There were supposed to be AGMs with Directors and Shareholders present. However, the notes from these meeting were scant and virtually all decisions seemed to taken by Rafi Razzak. A minimum number for the meetings was five which rarely seemed to materialise in the later years.

The Covenant was becoming a big issue. When the previous two attempts were made to move the club to Down Grange and the Old Common it was not such an issue. This was because the club would have moved into a new facility and few would have been bothered what happened at the Camrose. However in this situation the football club were to be displaced with a mitigation and the town would lose one of its two main football arenas.

CHAPTER 24

STOPPING THE UNSTOPPABLE

My week in politics was quite revealing. A few things had come out as virtually certain from the conversations I had. The first was this Proposal was 'unstoppable'. Everything had been approved. It was 'too late'. The second thing that came out was Basingstoke had a DIY Council. If you wanted something done you had to 'Do It Yourself'. I decided the best thing to do in the absence of any Councillor or MP support was to copy everyone in with my e-mails. As well as Steph Condon at the Council I copied in Ann Court, Paul Harvey and the local MP Maria Miller. I was later to add Councillor Stephen Reid, my Hampshire County Council contact. Also Neil

Cassar of the Hampshire Football Association.

My first e-mails were to explain to them that we were dealing with a full-blown scandal. Decisions had to be considered and fair to the townsfolk. Once again I emphasised the point that it was unacceptable to lose one of the two main football arenas worth £5 million plus for an enhancement worth £250K to Winklebury if Basron felt it appropriate. The timescales were that approval was to be given in August '19 , September '19 at the latest. No immediate feedback was coming from anywhere although Steph Condon and Maria Miller were at least acknowledging they actually received e-mails. Maria Miller took the issue up with both Sport England and the Football Foundation and sent replies. In my opinion there was too much emphasis on the 'mitigation'. Essentially all options had been explored but Winklebury was the only option. In general a mitigation is providing some sort of compensation for a loss. However, there would be no need for the mitigation if the loss did not happen. Besides, the mitigation was certainly worth a lot more than a £250K enhancement to the HFA Headquarters.

Monitoring on everything relating to the Proposal was important, and to follow information from the Community Club and the Council. The first sign that we had made an impact came with Terry Brown, the Community Club Chairman, pleading with Rafi Razzak on BBC South Today to release money for Winklebury. Razzak appeared on BBC South flanked by David Knight and Malcolm McPhail.

August came and went. Then Terry Brown put in a submission to the Council again pleading to Razzak to provide the money for Winklebury. However, within his submission was the acknowledgement on respecting Sport England. However, he claimed that Winklebury was the one-for-one option which clearly it was not. From this point on we started to make a number of very small gains. Costa Coffee at the West Ham Roundabout became a favourite meeting place as I discussed issues on Legal, Law, Detective,

Accounts and a Councillor.

Outside of that, thanks to the amazing ring of contacts that are known to the Partridge family and others all sorts of information came to the fore. We were making up ground with our protest.

September came and went. I had a few queries in regard to the Hampshire Football Association but they were soon cleared up by Neil Cassar, the CEO again at the Costa Coffee at West Ham. I will probably have to have shares in Costa Coffee at some stage!!

In October '19 a second Planning Application went in from Basron for a Care Home.

Outline application for the erection of a 70 Bedroom Care Home and 6 new Dwellings with associated access and external works, following the demolition of the existing Coral Bookmakers and part of the existing Basingstoke Town FC Clubhouse (all matters reserved except access).

On cue I sent in my customary protest and amazingly it was included with all the other protest comments. This was to be the only one of my protest letters that was reproduced by the Council.

OBJECTION TO PROPOSED CARE HOME DEVELOPMENT AT THE CAMROSE FOOTBALL GROUND Number 19/02889/out

I wish to object to the Planning application No. 19/02889/out To build a care Home to replace the Corals bookmakers and the Basingstoke Town Supporters Clubhouse. This latest Proposal put forward formed part of the original Proposal No 19/01110/out to build houses on the site. My objections are identical to that which has already been put forward to the original Proposal. The reason is the completely inadequate replacement football provision being offered. Winklebury is not a One for One replacement of football provision as the Camrose was and enjoyed by the Basingstoke football fraternity. It matters not whether Houses, a Care Home or a Turkish steam brothel is being put forward. The alternative has not been provided for the Camrose Ground. BASRON: Basron should be made to follow the advice of Sport England and the Football Foundation who have recommended that the proposal should be rejected. They should be offered a plot of land for sale where they can build a replacement football ground to Step 2 standard.

Note: The club played at Step 2 grade before the owner degraded the ground Once a new Basingstoke Club is playing football at the new venue, then and only then, should Planning Permission be provided for Development at the Camrose Ground.

COUNCIL: The Council should follow the advice of Sport England. Recommendations put forward by Sport England are accepted in 89% of cases. The 11% who do not comply soon find that their Sports provision is diminished. In addition Basingstoke Council should follow the lead given by Bury Council in the light of the Bury FC scandal. They immediately announced that no planning permission would be accepted until another identical standard ground was provided elsewhere in the town. When the original announcement in was made in 2017 about Winklebury a figure of £250K was put forward as being sufficient. This of course was absurd. The latest estimates are at £750K and still going up. The BTFC Ltd owner clearly has got his figures badly wrong and not for the first time. In 2010 he announced the club was debt free. Then in 2016 Companies House announced that the club were £1.4 million in debt. A man who dubs himself 'Mr. Spreadsheet'. Looking at his figures from Companies House over the years he probably meant 'Mr. Bedsheet'. Basingstoke has two main football arenas and I believe the town should retain two main football arena's. This would show a good commitment to sport in the time.

From: Mr. David Graham

A separate Planning Application went in from Hampshire County Council to build a loop road through the Camrose ground. This was to be part of the Brighton Hill roundabout scheme. I contacted our local County Councillor Stephen Reid. The answers provided were concise and very helpful. He handled the query in a very professional manner. In essence he indicated that the loop road would only happen if Basingstoke Council approved of the Camrose ground redevelopment. It was strange to receive a reply from a Councillor but it was very welcome.

Construction of a two-way single carriageway link between the existing Western Way/Buckland Ave mini roundabout through the former Basingstoke Football Ground and then onto A30 Winchester Road

PLEASE NOTE THAT THE DECISION ON THIS APPLICATION IS MADE BY HAMPSHIRE COUNTY COUNCIL

Basron were to gain a boost in regards to the HFA site at Winklebury. The long awaited planning permission went in from the Community Club supported by Basron. Rafi Razzak's Architects, Fabinacci from Dorking, had submitted the drawings. Of course it was odd that Basron were to be involved in any way at Winklebury with the HFA Redevelopment project. I was dismayed when it was approved by the Council. This Proposal was of course the mitigation award that was approved by the Football Foundation. However, huge question marks existed on how this project was going to be funded. The heading was:

ENHANCEMENT OF THE EXISTING FACILITIES AT THE WINKLEBURY FOOTBALL COMPLEX FOR BASINGSTOKE TOWN COMMUNITY FOOTBALL CLUB

So Christmas was reached and it was safe to say the Unstoppable had been Stopped and hopefully for ever. Things were to take many dramatic turns thereafter!!

STEPHEN REID

CHAPTER 25

RESEEDING THE CAMROSE

The year 2020 arrived. A year that no one will ever forget with the unfolding tragedy and despair due to the coronavirus pandemic.

Rafi Razzak was getting desperate. The Basron Proposal was beginning to stall. He was putting pressure on the Community Club to try and achieve an acceptance of Winklebury as a solution. The slogan was 'Get the boys back to Basingstoke'. Razzak had commissioned Architects to try and push things along a bit by carrying out Design work for the Winklebury return. It was unsure who gave approval for Fabinacci Architects to go ahead with it. Probably 'jumping the gun'.

However, it was his next act to force things through that caused fury throughout the town. He brought in diggers to start digging up the Camrose pitch. There was an almighty uproar. The townsfolk had finally realised that they were to lose one of their cherished venues in the town. The reason given for this action was initially that it was to pave the way for the loop road through the Camrose as per the Hampshire County Council Proposal. However, it had already been established that the road could not progress until Basingstoke Council had approved the Camrose Development. The work was eventually brought to a halt. Razzak gave his explanation to the Basingstoke Gazette's Beth Whittingham.

Speaking to the Gazette, Mr Razzak said workers were 'removing the top soil' in preparation to lay new turf.

He said: "I was completely unaware of it at first, but I can confirm that they are not tearing down the football pitch, they are simply removing the top soil.

"We have taken the football posts away because the football team no longer use this football ground, they haven't been sold they're just in storage."

The Camrose stadium was the home of Basingstoke Town Football Club for more than 70 years until the club were evicted in August.

They have been playing at Winchester ever since while the side's future remains uncertain.

The planning application originally offered 89 new houses with a hotel, a restaurant and a care home which has now been revised to just host the houses and care home development as a wider part of redevelopment of Brighton Hill.

Mr Razzak added: "We expected the planning permission to have been approved by now which is why the Basingstoke Town Football Club left at the beginning of the season, so far it has been postponed but we will get the planning permission approved shortly."

The pressure was now on to get the Camrose ground saved and restored as a football ground. Events were moving quickly helped in no small way by the fantastic coverage in the local media. Something that had been sadly missing on some occasions previously. The Basingstoke Gazette Investigative Journalism Department was moving into top gear.

More extraordinary things were about to unfold.

CHAPTER 26

THE COVENANT IS FOUND

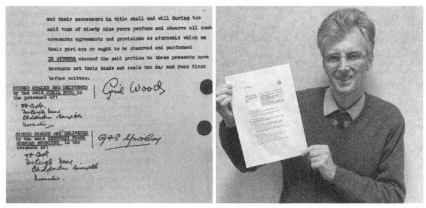

GRAHAM MERRY –

BASINGSTOKE GAZETTE WITH THE COVENANT

They say if you pray hard enough amazing things happen!!

With the reseeding project of the Camrose in full swing there was to be another huge setback for Rafi Razaak. Through amazing detective work the Lord Camrose Covenant was found. This sparked a huge outpouring of comment to the Basingstoke Gazette for their headline. At the Council meetings in 2017 the claim was made that the Covenant was lost. This was as a riposte to the content within the Lord Camrose Covenant. In other words, 'Shucks. Bad luck, guys!! Unless the actual document is produced to see the actual wording, well there is nothing we can do!! We will carry on trying to find this elusive document. No stone will be left unturned!!'

It was easy to see why Basron wanted the Covenant lost. It was there in black and white. The ground was left to Basingstoke for use as a sports facility for 100 years; 2053 was when the lease runs out.

The Gazette article read:

A HISTORIC document that states that the former home of Basingstoke Town Football Club must remain as a sports facility until 2053 has been unearthed.

For years, the public and the press have been told that the covenant put in place by Lord Camrose to protect the Camrose ground had been 'lost' or in some cases 'didn't exist'.

However this week, this newspaper can exclusively reveal the covenant is very much still in existence. In papers obtained by the Gazette, the covenant can be clearly viewed on the Land Registry paperwork which states the Winchester Road site must remain as a football ground.

In the document, signed in 1953 by Lord William Berry, Viscount Camrose, it states:

No buildings or erection shall be planned or allowed on the land which is a Football or Sports Ground.

Not to erect or permit to be erected on the said land any buildings without the written consent of the lessors and the tenants can only erect building connected with purpose already mentioned above.

Not to carry on or permit to be carried on any trade or business upon the said land only to use or allow to permit the same to be used in a proper and orderly manner as a Football or Sports Ground which is purpose of this lease

Not to do or permit any act or thing which causes or may grow to cause annoyance inconvenience nuisance of any neighbouring property.

Driving cattle, sheep and other animals cannot be done on the land which is marked out as a football pitch.

The agreement between Lord Camrose and the then owners of Basingstoke Town

Football Club says that the land, "laid out for the playing of football", must be a "football or sports ground" throughout the period of the covenant, with "no buildings or erection ... placed or allowed to remain on the land."

It continues to say that no business should be allowed on the land other than a football ground. However, after Basingstoke Town Football Club owner Rafi Razzak's company Centerprise purchased the freehold to the ground in 2016, there is now a dispute about whether the covenant still applies.

Tim Crarer, senior partner at law firm Parker Bullen, said that it was "quite a complicated situation".

He says that there are a few methods how covenants can be attacked, by deeming it obsolete if it has not been enforced, by deeming it no longer appropriate, and if it has already been released by the owner.

As Mr Razzak now owns the football club and the ground, he is landlord and tenant, and on both sides of the covenant, says Basingstoke and Deane Borough Council's deputy leader Simon Bound.

Cllr Bound told the Gazette: "There was a covenant between Lord Camrose and the football club. "I have asked this point over and over again to the football club, they have sought legal advice that it doesn't stand."

He says that regardless of whether it is valid or not, it will likely not be enforced by Mr Razzak. Cllr Bound added that a board member of the community club told fans at a meeting he attended around 18 months ago to "forget the covenant", saying it will not protect football at the Camrose.

The covenant has been thought of as potential ammunition that could see the town's club return to its historic home. This has led to the community club's director, Kevin White, to say he was "shocked" that the covenant has been found and could still be valid.

"When Rafi purchased it, he removed it without anybody knowing. My understanding is that the land was sold with the intention that the covenant remained.

"If it is still valid then it makes the situation worse and even more callous really.

"I am quite shocked that if it says it is still valid. I can only assume that they can do what they want with the covenant."

As previously reported, the pitch at the former home of the town's club was ripped up last month, with owner Rafi Razzak saying he wasn't aware that it was taking place.

He has submitted plans that would see retail units built on the site, and told the Gazette that the grass was being re-seeded.

However, Mr Razzak has called debate over the covenant "ridiculous".

He said: "It has saddened me that it has come to this after 22 years at the football club. What would I gain with that support for 20 years?

"The money I put down was to help the club to build a stadium at National League standard.

"I did it for the right reasons for the football club and the community, like everything else I have done.

"There is not future at the Camrose. The club needed £100,000 a year to continue to play at the Camrose which I funded myself for 20 years. I have had enough of funding the club."

Councillor Bounds asserted that as Rafi Razzak is at both sides of the Covenant and he can do as he likes. That is untrue on several fronts. Firstly there is no doubt that Basron purchased the ground from Camrose Estates. There is also no doubt that the ground was sold with the Covenant on it as David Partridge outlined to the Council in 2017. The documents at the Land Registry office prove that. The land was purchased for £2.4 million with a Covenant on it. Without a Covenant on the land a development for housing would be worth around £5 million.

There is a complication that the two Aldermen who received the Covenant were also Trustees of the football club. However, it would be churlish to imply that the Camrose ground was decided not to be for the benefit of the populace of Basingstoke. It was definitely not scheduled to be converted into Houses and a Care Home 70 years later. It would be the most tenuous technicality to suggest that the ground was to be the total preserve of the football club. Even if somehow this argument is accepted it would imply that the Covenant should continue along the same path and hence be handed over to the Community Club.

In the setting up of Basingstoke Town Ltd, Phillips the Solicitors drafted up a 35-page set of conditions. Nowhere is there any indication that the Covenant was transferred from the original Basingstoke Town Football and Social Club Ltd. This is surely a key detail in the transfer between the clubs. As it turns out, Basingstoke Town Football and Social Club Ltd did not stop trading until 2005. It would be ludicrous to suggest that two clubs were walking around with the Covenant in their pocket. The whole situation is an absolute mess and the fairest course of action is for the ground to remain as a venue for sporting activities. Having destroyed the ground in an act of mindless vandalism, Razzak should be required to replace it. It is accepted that Phillips the Solicitors acted on two sides of the Covenant; Basingstoke Town FC Ltd and Basron Ltd.

A second and more important point which does not seem to have been picked up by any Councillor is 'Conflict of Interest'. The Definition of 'Conflict of Interest is given as:

What Is a Conflict of Interest?

A conflict of interest occurs when an entity or individual becomes unreliable because of a clash between personal (or self-serving) interests and professional duties or responsibilities. Such a conflict occurs when a company or person has a vested interest, such as money, status, knowledge, relationships, or reputation, which puts into question whether their actions, judgment, and/or decision-making can be unbiased. When such a situation arises, the party is usually asked to remove themselves, and it is often legally required of them.

In the case of the Camrose Scandal there is surely a blatant three-way 'Conflict of Interest' involving Rafi Razzak. He has control of the three of the main parties involved in the scandal:

1) He is the owner of Centerprise, the main sponsor to Basingstoke Town Football Club Ltd. Centerprise set up Basron as the Developer of the Camrose ground. Razzak owns 50% of Basron Ltd. Centerprise provided Basron Ltd with the £2.4 million which was used to purchase the Camrose.

2) Razzak is joint owner of Basron Ltd with Malcolm McPhail. Basron Ltd are the Developer seeking to build on the Camrose.

3) Razzak is owner of Basingstoke Town FC Ltd and appears to wish the club to cease trading with his submissions to the Council. The last set of figures submitted to Companies House showed the club in debt to the tune of £1.4 million.

It is understood that the principle of being involved with multiple companies is acceptable. It becomes unacceptable when one or more of the companies gains considerably at the expense of one or more of the other identities. In these cases it is often against the law and can lead to prosecution. Clearly Basingstoke Town FC Ltd were badly disadvantaged to the benefit of Razzak and Basron Ltd.

The Councillors were starting to be under a fair bit of scrutiny and the Community Club had a major setback when the founder Steve Williams announced he was stepping down. It would be true to say that Williams had absolutely no chance from day 1. A statement from Terry Brown announced his departure.

Steve Williams

On behalf of the Community Club Board, I am sad to announce that for personal reasons Steve Williams has decided to stand down from his role as Club Secretary and board member. Steve and Denise have always been much more than secretary or volunteer board members. They have been a massive driving force, that has allowed us to take over the running of our football club. A club that survives financially without any help from the massive corporations we are dealing with on a day to day basis.

Steve has agreed to continue supporting our planning application, where his expertise and diligence are crucial to our aim of returning home.

Personally I would like to put on record my appreciation of everything Steve has done for our club. He has guided me and helped me to adjust into the role of Chairman. He has written our Business Plan and supervised a budget without the help of the necessary revenue streams to run a football club. He has also managed to navigate a pathway between HFA, their builders SIS and Malcolm McPhail co-director of Basron who ejected us from the Camrose. Add to this the cocktail of love between the Council and (I won't let the club die) RAFI, and you get some idea what a job he has done working alongside every party that claims to be helping our club move into Winklebury. (Henry Kissinger: Eat Your Heart Out).

Many thanks to a lovely couple, who will always be warmly welcomed to Winklebury.

Regards
Terry Brown

Chairman Of Basingstoke Town Community Football Club

Steve Williams was to subsequently state at the Council meeting that Winklebury could only ever be a short-term mitigation for the loss of the Camrose.

CHAPTER 27

BASINGSTOKE COUNCILLORS

The discovery of the Covenant switched the focus on to the local councillors. The Gazette article below gives their views on the find.

PAUL MILLER NICHOLAS ROBINSON STEPHANIE GRANT

THE *discovery of a covenant designed to protect a football ground from being built on has raised questions about whether permission can be granted to turn the site into a housing estate.*

Basingstoke and Deane Borough Council's development control committee will be making a decision about whether 88 homes can be built on top of Basingstoke Town Football Club's former home in April.

Last year, a planning application on behalf of Basron Developments was submitted to build houses and a care home at the Camrose stadium on Winchester Road. It came after the football club was evicted from the Camrose.

Earlier this month, the Gazette uncovered a covenant - which the council previously claimed 'didn't exist' – which showed the intent of the original landowner Lord Camrose was for the ground to remain a sports facility until 2053.

Its discovery has thrown legal and ethical questions into the mix with Basingstoke Town Football Club currently seeking advice about what this means.

Ahead of the planning decision this spring, reporters contacted those on the authority's development control committee (also known as a planning committee) for their view on the plight of the football club and whether the covenant should be upheld.

There are 12 members on the committee and eleven were available to comment. Out of the group, only Cllr Stephanie Grant (Labour, Buckskin) expressed disappointment that the covenant was not being respected.

Three members said they 'didn't care' about football and didn't have an opinion on the plight of the football club.

Cllr Grant said: "I think Lord Camrose would be very disappointed with what has happened to the Camrose, it's been there for as long as I have but it's got to the stage now where it's Winklebury or die for the football club."

Cllr Michael Bound (Lib Dem, Baughurst and Tadley North) said the covenant happened a long time ago and said homelessness was more of a concern. He said: "[The covenant] happened a very long time ago, some 70 years ago, Lord Camrose wouldn't have known how the town has developed, he couldn't have foreseen it."

"When we're short of money as a council, I think issues like homelessness are a bigger concern."

Cllr Nicholas Robinson (Conservative, Bramley and Sherfield) said: "I don't know what I'm talking about. Leave me out of it, I'm on the slopes."

Chairman of the committee, Cllr Paul Miller (Conservative, Chineham) said he had little interest in football. He said: "I have a little bit of an international background and the one thing I take no interest in is English soccer. I am a *rugby man."*

Cllr David Leeks (Conservative, Tadley South) said: "I haven't got a clue. I am not interested in football at all."

When asked whether he thought Basingstoke Town Football Club should be moved back to Basingstoke, he said: "I have taken no interest in it, I have plenty of other things going on."

When asked if he could put his personal interests aside and speak on behalf of the town, he said: "When it comes to planning, I'll read the papers diligently and make a decision."

The development and control board will begin discussions on the planning permission at the beginning of April.

Cllr David Potter (Independent, Popley East) said the council had the power to help the club if they wanted but questioned why they hadn't previously.

He said: "This is a rich council and I think we forget that sometimes. They have just opened the new Village Hotel which cost £3 million and they bought B&Q from an American billionaire for £7.5 million so don't tell me they can't do it.

"They can clearly do it if they want to and I think they have the power to move it forward if they want to and this applies to the ice rink and other sporting facilities."

Cllr Andrew McCormick (Labour, Brighton Hill) said there was 'no time' to fight for the Camrose. He said Winklebury was the only option.

He said he wanted the Brighton Hill roundabout development to go ahead, which would mean building on the Camrose.

The development control board will begin discussions on the planning permission at the beginning of April.

Who are councillors and what do they do?

Councillors are publicly-elected politicians that represent the public at local level. They receive an allowance from the taxpayer that varies depending on their responsibilities. They can also claim expenses.

Having learned about the way the Basingstoke Executive carried out their operations I began to have some sympathy with the work the local Councillors carry out. That is, providing they represent the wards to the best of their ability. I feel certain the majority of them do.

As I have already alluded there does not appear to be much in the way of representation from the Councillors in my ward, Kempshott. I cannot believe that this is typical, it is just my bad luck living where I do. The leader of the Council does not want to speak with me; well, I suppose that is fair enough, he is probably a busy man. However, some of the responses from the Councillors in respect to the Camrose Scandal and the finding of the Covenant were bizarre. This is picked up in the letter from Adrian Donnelly.

I was astounded reading the comments from our elected councillors in last week's *Gazette*. How did these people get elected?

"I don't know what I'm talking about."

"I am a rugby man."

"I haven't got a clue, as I'm not interested in football."

"When we are short of money, homelessness is more important."

Firstly, what should be paramount to every councillor is the wellbeing of the community that they are serving. That wellbeing includes a town football club.

Secondly, the Gazette reported a few months ago, the Basingstoke council where in the richest half of councils in England. So what has happened since October 2019?

Have all the funds gone on golden goodbyes, as the council is top of this list as well! Another Gazette scoop.

Everywhere you look around Basingstoke, there are houses being built , offices blocks being converted, and planning permission given for more houses.

The council must be adding social housing to all these developments. The golf club, opposite the golf club, Manydown, etc. Homelessness will always be there, at some level.

The council's job is to balance all requirements. A newspaper report recently stated there are over one million houses in England, that have had planning permission granted, but not yet built. I wonder how many of those are in Basingstoke.

With all this increased population we need community facilities, whether it is a replacement ice rink, a new football ground, or a bigger and better rugby clubhouse.

Coming back to the Camrose scandal, the council will not need to spend taxpayers new money on rehousing the football, if the covenant is proved to be worthless. It owns 30% of the football ground.

If we cannot get Camrose restored, it can use the money that it will receive from that sale, to build a new stadium, fit for a town which will be breaking 200,000 population in the near future.

Get a grip councillors, and do your job properly, as it is taxpayers money that covers your salaries, pensions, and golden goodbyes!

As for Mr Razzak, a person worth over £90 million, perhaps he should stop trying to add to his wealth at 70 years of age, and think wouldn't it be good to leave a legacy to the town that took me in, and give us back our ground.

I would be happy to rename it, Razzak stadium. Write off your "investment", and be remembered for something good.

Adrian Donnelly

Adrian Donnelly's views reflect that of the vast bulk of the Basingstoke populace. The one which probably reflects how out of touch they are is the comment of Councillor Paul Miller of Chineham. It is one thing not to be interested in football. However, it is pretty shabby in light of the tremendous reputation Chineham football teams have had over the years. When my sons played, Chineham Park Rangers were a force in boys football. Chineham were one of the clubs nominated to use the HFA complex at Winklebury. Nowadays we have Chineham Tigers who have a host of boys and girls teams who go out every weekend and play football. The coaches give up their time to give instruction. It gives the parents an interest and football is good for both the character and physical wellbeing of the boys and girls. They have a popular and well-run Sunday side in the Basingstoke League. That does not seem to matter to Councillor Miller. He is just not interested in football.

However, he is keen to mix with someone who has an interest in football. He was present when Rafi Razaak unveiled the fighter jet in honour of his father. I believe it is important for a Councillor to get involved in all aspects of the community they represent. Clearly football is important and the Camrose Scandal needs to be thought through and resolved.

It is true to say that sometimes a minority of football fans give the sport a tarnished image. However, they are a very small minority compared to the vast numbers that participate each weekend in sport. All sports give people an interest and enjoyment in taking part and spectating. Part of our Community Charge goes to sport. Sport England is the lottery funding. I believe those that say they have no interest in aspects of sport are effectively saying they are not interested in the people they represent.

A hypothetical comparison would be what would happen if Rafi Razzak was involved at the Anvil. He joins a group support and eventually after a few years finishes being responsible for the funding. He runs the hall down until springs are coming out of the seats, the toilets not kept up and the air conditioning does not work. The charges remain high but no real top-notch performers come. The attendances drop with people going to Reading and Southampton to watch performances. Razzak discovers that there is a Covenant on the Anvil ground left when the previous land owners the Civil Service moved out. He buys the land and then wants the Anvil moved to a local district Community Hall. The Council say all the Arts and Music fans must form into a Community Group and help upgrade the Community Hall. Mr Razzak must be allowed to build on the Anvil; it is after all his land.

Would those that are anti-football take the same view with the Anvil comparison? I think not and rightly so. The Anvil represents what is good in Basingstoke and so should the Camrose. Basingstoke should be offering quality for football, ice hockey and all other sports.

THE ANVIL – BASINGSTOKE

CHAPTER 28

THE PROTESTERS GAIN SUPPORT

CLUB LEGEND BILLY COOMBS SCORES THE WINNER
AGAINST BROMLEY

The Basingstoke Gazette were at the forefront of the protests. Good articles appeared including a quote from Gary Lineker, the BBC presenter. Graham Merry appeared on BBC South. A grandson of Lord Camrose commented that he was aware of the protests.

Then a huge boost came in for the Protesters. The ex-Basingstoke Town footballers' group which has around 300 members offered to help us. Suddenly from being a marginal voice of protest the whole situation was quickly turning around.

Two petitions drew around 2,500 signatures. The slogan was 'Save the Camrose – No to Winklebury'. The Gazette organised two protests at the Camrose ground. Despite atrocious weather both had decent turnouts. The visit to the ground left everyone sad. How any owner of a club could systematically degrade the ground over so many years was unbelievable. Then to destroy it was unforgivable.

It was a pleasure to get support from such an important group. They turned out to very supportive from the start. Adrian Donnelly was a former All Blacks player in the Basingstoke Sunday League. They were virtually untouchable in their time and the Camrose was their second home as they turned up to play in Cup Finals. His contributions were always thoughtful and accurate. Steve Frangou I remember from when they won the league in the 1980s. Amazingly, that was the last time the club actually won a league. I helped Steve with the Youth set up for a short period before he left to join Fred Callaghan, the former Fulham player at another club. However, it was nice meeting Billy Coombs and I gave him the updates when our paths crossed at Sainsbury's Kempshott. Billy was a legend at the club. He played for many seasons and was probably the first name on the team sheet each week. The midfielder was always a fan favourite and a contender for Player of the Season on most occasions. There were countless others all with their memories of the town's football ground. Colin Stoker was a totally composed character having been involved in virtually every capacity at the club. He was a Player, a Manager and a Director and a great influence in the background debates.

It was this group which added a lot of quality to the Council Chambers debate in February 2020 on the Basingstoke Town situation. Steve Frangou, Colin Stoker, Adrian Donnelly and former Community Club board member Steve Williams all spoke well. The Council advised that they would consult Sport England in respect to getting the One-for-One replacement. All agreed that any move to Winklebury could only be a very short one. Restoring the Camrose or a One-for-One replacement is urgently required.

The comments in the Basingstoke Gazette clearly show a desire for the town to have the Camrose back. Katie French, the relatively new editor at the Gazette, has certainly pushed the newspaper into being more challenging. They have kept the Camrose Scandal issue at the fore and each development has provoked much comment. One group which has not offered much in the way of support for a return to the Camrose is the Community Club. They probably see themselves as part of the Collaboration and have stuck steadfastly to getting the 'mitigation' first and the Camrose replacement later. Graham Merry left the Gazette at the end of March 2020 after a very long stint as the senior sports editor. His knowledge of the local sporting scene is considerable with a vast number of sports covered. He will be a very hard act to follow.

ADRIAN DONNELLY (LEFT), STEVE FRANGOU (CENTRE)

CHAPTER 29

FOOTBALL GROUND SCANDALS

Football ground scandals are of course not new. They have been happening for at least the last three decades. It is tempting for a sharp businessperson to get involved in a football club and offer some sort of financial support. Many of the grounds are on land that has enormous potential for development and the hence ideal for making a substantial profit. Many if not most football clubs probably run at a deficit. If the debt runs up it is tempting to accept the offer of financial help. The seemingly kind benefactor can then influence decisions with the power of his apparent wealth. The initial goal is get into the top position and from there the ground ownership comes into focus.

The Football Association are aware of this and over the years have put guidelines in place to try and prevent this sort of thing happening. Sport England is a Statutory body and offers guidance to Local Authorities with Planning Applications. The Football Foundation who distribute the money for ground improvements also give recommendations.

The Basingstoke Town situation is the worst scandal ever in non-league football. Perhaps two other cases are worth considering.

ENFIELD FC – SOUTHBURY ROAD

ENFIELD FC

Enfield were a highly successful non-league club over a long period of time. By coincidence the first time I watched Enfield play was in 1964, a year after I moved down from Scotland. The match was an Amateur Cup Final and it was against Crook Town at Wembley. Enfield were the better side in the first half and led 1-0 at the break. Unfortunately for them in the pre-substitute days the goalie got injured and Crook Town took advantage to win 2-1. Over the years I watched them many times against Slough Town and Basingstoke Town. Slough in fact signed a number of Enfield players when manager Tommy Lawrence moved to Slough. Alf D'arcey, Joe Adams, keeper Wolstenholme and winger Hill helped Slough to a successful period. Enfield were always a force; usually in the higher divisions. Great Cup fighters over the years including the FA Cup.

A scandal took place between two and three decades ago involving Enfield FC. This has a number of similarities to Basingstoke Town. A local Estate Agent called Tony Lazarou joined the club in 1991 and offered financial support at a time when the club was on the low point of its cash flow cycle. In return for his 'investment' Lazarou managed to get into a position of influence and quickly became Chairman and Owner. The problem started with a potential business opportunity. Saracens the Rugby Union club were looking to have a bigger venue to cope with their increased attendances. To accommodate the 'Saries' one side of the ground had to be flattened and replaced with a temporary stand with much scaffolding. This gave Enfield a decent income from the ground hire. Unfortunately it was to only last for one year. Saracens were given the opportunity to move to Vicarage Road at Watford which they accepted. Enfield had to dismantle the temporary stand erected for the Saracens. This left the ground content at a lower level than the FA requirements and hampered and chance of the club progressing upwards.

Tony Lazarou, to the disgust of the Enfield faithful decided to put the ground up for sale to developers during 1999. Southbury Road was sold for £750K for Development, a seemingly low figure, and the club were homeless. They moved around several grounds including Boreham Wood. However, the supporters were unhappy with events – not surprisingly – and formed a Trust. Lazarou promised the club £100K to £200K as an ongoing payment which he refused to honour. The FA stepped in and instructed the Council to ensure he paid the £200K. Lazarou threatened to sue the Council if they pressed for the money and the weak Enfield Council buckled. Enfield Town were formed and started to play at Brimsdown in the Essex League. Enfield Town moved back up the leagues and have now reached the Isthmian Premier level. They have moved back into the Enfield Borough and the Queen Elizabeth Stadium which is near the old Southbury Road ground.

The original Enfield FC continued in the hope that Lazarou would pay the outstanding monies they were owed. They played at Ware and a few other venues. However, Lazarou refused to pay up and the club became defunct. They were offered a merger with Enfield Town but turned it down. In 2007 they reformed as Enfield 1893 and play at Brimsdown. Having started at a low level they have moved up a few notches but Enfield Town have the bulk of the support.

Tony Lazarou was subsequently banned for life for all football involvement by the Football Association. In 2019 it is believed he was declared Bankrupt.

GIGG LANE – BURY

BURY FC

The Camrose Scandal is not the only one in progress at the moment. Bury FC have a parallel scandal involving the potential development of their Gigg Lane ground. In short, the owner of Bury FC wanted to sell the ground for development, supposedly to clear debts. Steve Dale had only taken over the club in December 2018 from Stewart Day. He was soon to find that the club's debts were huge and the only way out of the mire was to sell Gigg Lane. Bury had actually won promotion in season 2018-19 to EFL Division 1. As a consequence the club were expelled from the Football League at the start of season 2019-20.

The difference between the approach taken by the Bury Council and the Basingstoke Council is chalk to cheese. The Bury Councillors, MP and townsfolk have acted as one and been proactive from the start. Bury Council immediately stepped in and said the ground must not be sold for development until the issue regarding Gigg Lane was resolved. The supporters reformed the club and have entered the non-league pyramid. They are planning on playing at Radcliffe. The Bury Conservative MP James Daly used his maiden speech in the House of Commons to highlight the Bury FC scandal. He has been very active in pursuing it ever since. Bury FC will be back.

By contrast, Basingstoke Council have been inactive in resolving the problem. It first surfaced in 2017 when there were protests by the fans and representations to the Council. The fact it has surfaced again three years later is frankly appalling.

A select group at the House of Commons provided the content of this article.

An inquiry set up following the recent scandal at Bury FC has led to calls for "urgent action" to prevent other clubs experiencing the same fate as the Shakers, who were removed from the EFL earlier this year.

Today the DCMS committee has written to Sports Minister Nigel Adams, EFL executives and the FA laying out their recommendations.

These include the FA, EFL and Premier League introducing a supporters' ombudsman to hear concerns about how clubs are being run.

An independent ombudsman already exists to investigate complaints that are not resolved by the aforementioned bodies, yet it has little power.

MPs have also called for a reformed Owners' and Directors' Test – a bone of contention for Blackpool fans in recent years – that would disqualify a prospective buyer of a club with a record of corporate insolvency.

The DCMS committee has also wrote to the EFL demanding a formal apology to staff and supporters at Bury, with reparations made for associated loss of earnings. If these recommendations were enforced, clubs would also be banned from borrowing against fixed assets such as stadiums. DCMS chair Damian Collins MP said: "Systematic and structural problems are responsible for the tragic expulsion of Bury FC from the League this year.

"These failures were avoidable and it is essential that the authorities urgently overhaul their framework if they wish to avoid the same fate befalling other clubs.

"We heard time and again that supporters felt powerless as they watched their beloved club suffer shocking mismanagement and financial misconduct. "The authorities must learn to respect, and act upon, these concerns. If the reforms we recommend are not introduced forthwith, the only alternative is for the government to step in." MPs found the problems at Bury preceded the tenure of the current owner Steve Dale, and say the EFL must share the blame for having allowed the situation at the club to have deteriorated for so long.

During the inquiry, the DCMS claim it found compelling evidence of "failings at every level of football governance". This is something that has long been argued by Blackpool supporters, who were left furious by the lack of action during their battle with despised former owner Owen Oyston.

Pool fans have long campaigned for change in the way football is run, previously launching a petition calling on the government to introduce an independent regulator.

There was an all-party Parliamentary group for football set up in 2008. They got a report commissioned by Birkbeck at the University of London.

It is lengthy with many sensible recommendations.

Although the FA have moved a long way in addressing the scandals they need to be given more powers of enforcement.

CHAPTER 30

TOWARDS A CONCLUSION

KATIE FRENCH –

BASINGSTOKE GAZETTE

Into June 2020 and the Community Club issued a statement. I went out to my back garden and looked to the skies and said, 'Hallelujah! May the Lord be praised!!' After three years the Community Club finally had come round to our way of thinking.

As many of you will know; there are ongoing negotiations between Basingstoke & Deane Borough Council, Basron and Sport England regarding the much needed compensation to be paid to the town via the 'Section 106' ruling for the loss of The Camrose facility.

Chairman Terry Brown & Vice Chairman Kevin White, on behalf of the club and supporters, are unwavered in their pursuit to ensure a second stadium remains in the town; not only for the clubs longer term aspirations but also to ensure the town does not lose a facility.

Vice Chairman Kevin White said recently 'I feel almost embarrassed saying it as it's so blindingly obvious that there is a desperate need to re-establish another ground in the town. I really cannot see a debate? Other towns have incorporated new office spaces into new facilities and it's worked incredibly well. With a town our size, coupled with the plans in the councils Horizon 2050 document, I am in no doubt that it can be done here too.'

Chairman Terry Brown echoed this approach and believes that the true cost of a proper, long term facility is upward of £4m.

'I have been in football a long time and a stadium is more than just a football pitch – and quite rightly so. They now incorporate retail space, office units, training pitches – the possibilities and potential are endless. So as you can imagine, with a town of our size, this could be something truly special. The plans the council has needs to look past just football and think about how it will best serve the community. Let's not forget the positive impact football has on local communities, not just for those that are lucky enough to play the game, but the hundreds of children that come through the gates to watch, parents who are given the opportunity to share something with their kids, the elderly, our disabled community – it's a huge existing network already, but it needs to be given the chance to flourish.'

He continues 'If we use Avely FC as an example – they have a facility that was £4m-£5m to build. Melksham FC, who are in our league, together with the council they married together football and rugby and their new facility cost somewhere in the region of £7m. The same can be said for over at Dartford FC. Maybe looking at a home for the football club and the rugby club is a potential answer, we want sport in general to flourish in the town so the more we can work in partnership the better, but either way, something needs to be done, and quickly.'

Kevin White followed up by saying 'this shouldn't be seen as a cost, it should be seen as a long term investment in the infrastructure of the town. Done correctly, the return on investment could be significant, it can be funded in part or whole by Basron and Hampshire County Council and will help all aspects of the town in line with Horizon 2050. History will be watching this moment. Clubs, supporters and sport in general up and down the country will be looking at our story. A town likes ours that boasts about its plans for the future. It's a great message, but the proof will be in the action taken.'

The Camrose Scandal has been an unmitigated disaster for the Basingstoke football fraternity. The fact it has spanned two decades is really unforgivable. The central character to this is of course Rafi Razaak. The Enfield scandal was awful but it lasted for less than one decade.

At the end of my two-minute presentation in July 2017 to the Council I said, 'I do not agree to this!!' This was in reference to the Community Club and Council push to get to Winklebury. At the conclusion the Winklebury proposers seemed happy as they shook hands and patted backs.

February 2020 saw a return to the Council Chambers. I was allowed one question and one follow-up question. My question was, 'Were the Council aware that in accepting a £250K enhancement to Winklebury in exchange for the Camrose they would be losing one of the two main football arenas?' Councillor Simon Bounds did not answer the question. Instead he said that Alan Turvey was a much respected man. Also that as Rafi Razaak was now both sides of the Covenant he could do what he wished. I told him his answer was rubbish, as explained in Chapter 26. I then asked why Basron were doing work at Winklebury and if there was a Council Tender process.

As I write I have learned that Sport England, a respected Statutory body, have once again savaged the Basron attempts to get planning permission. They have put a time limit on the Winklebury development to end at July 2021. In addition they have told Basron that they must pay £300K for the loss of the two training courts at the Camrose. Also another £100K for the loss of the main grass pitch. They have also said they must pay compensation for the loss of the Camrose to the Council. This was followed by the Community

Club announcing that they will support the push for a One-for-One replacement for the Camrose. It is a pity they did not take this stance in 2017. Another small positive is that the Council have announced that they have rejected Hampshire County Council's proposal to put a loop road through the Camrose.

How will it finish? I think things are going in the right direction but with an extremely weak Council things are likely to be slow. In the meantime Basingstoke Town supporters will be travelling to Winchester. A town with a massive population playing their fixtures outside the borough against in some cases village sides in Devon, Somerset and Gloucestershire.

It is said that people in Basingstoke are not interested in football. This is untrue. There is no reason why people in Basingstoke should be any less interested in football than towns anywhere else. If a good match day experience is put on in a quality stadium then the fans will come. Woking, Farnborough, Eastleigh and many others have developed good grounds over the past two decades. The owner of Basingstoke Town allowed the Camrose ground to be degraded and then finished up destroying it. This a ground that was left to the Basingstoke public by Lord Camrose.

One obvious solution to the problem would be for Basingstoke Council to allocate a plot of land to Basron of the same value and size as the Camrose. Allow Basron to build a One-for-One redeveloped stadium at the Camrose for £4 to £5 million. Once the team is back in their new stadium playing then give approval to Basron to build houses on the land provided to them However, it is probably too obvious to Basingstoke Council who would rather spend further time going around on some other complex Collaboration agreement.

One aspect that has been a huge positive is the improvement in the journalism of the Basingstoke Gazette. Katie French leads a set of young enthusiastic journalists that are willing to take issue's on. Previous Gazette editors never really put in the same sort of challenge to the many topics that arose. The paper was often compared to a parish magazine.

Like the rest of the townsfolk I yearn for the day when we can get back to being like any other normal town. Take pride in our football ground and be ambassadors for Basingstoke.

CHAPTER 31

THE PROTESTERS CONTINUE TO GAIN

RAFI RAZZAK

June 2020 saw a few notable events.

The first was the departure of David Knight, the long-time senior figure at Basingstoke Town Ltd. In his time he was a good programme editor and held a few posts on the board of the Basingstoke Town Football and Social Club committee. However, he will probably be remembered unfortunately as Rafi Razzak's right-hand man on football matters. In July 2019 he appeared alongside Razzak on a BBC South item and his popularity took a severe dent with many of the fans.

Then two Council meetings on successive evenings proved interesting. A Scrutiny Committee was set up to try and establish the history of the events surrounding Basingstoke Town FC. Councillors Ian Tilbury and Paul Harvey tried to obtain answers but were out of luck.

The second meeting was for the Community and Environment Partnership. During the meeting a number of Councillors speaking expressed concern about the plight of the club. Clearly Winklebury could only be a short-term option and a way forward had to be sought. From the Protesters' point of view it was déjà vu. We had explained that to them in 2017 and they went along with the grand collaboration which has resulted in an almighty mess.

Local MP Maria Miller gave a boost to the Protesters with a welcome call for the replacement stadium.

BASINGSTOKE'S MP is calling on the council to ensure a like-for-like replacement for the Camrose is agreed before any development goes ahead.

Maria Miller has asked that a replacement sports ground for Basingstoke Town Football Club is assured.

It comes as the Camrose stadium, on Winchester Road, is subjected to two planning applications.

Hampshire Highways is seeking permission to build a road through the heart of the historic football ground, gifted to the town of Basingstoke in the 1950s by philanthropist Lord William Camrose.

While Basron Developers, owned by former Basingstoke Town chief executive Rafi Razzak, is hoping to turn the site into a housing development of 70+ homes.

Speaking ahead of Hampshire County Council's meeting to discuss the project to build a road through the site on Thursday, July 2, Maria said she wishes to be clear that the formal planning objection made by Sport England needs to be resolved in full before this road project moves forward.

Maria said: "Sport England has been clear from the start of this lengthy process that the owners of the Camrose ground have to make up for its loss before any redevelopment of the grounds can start.

"It was regrettable that the owners of the Camrose grounds decided to stop football being played there well before a new home for the team could be found.

"Now the owners of the ground need to do the right thing and put in place a legal undertaking to pay for the team to move to a new and suitably fitted out location."

Councillor Rob Humby, Deputy Leader and Executive Member for Economy, Transport and Environment at Hampshire County Council said: "We continue to work with Basingstoke and Deane Borough Council through the planning system to ensure that extra sports facilities are part of the planning agreement.

"We have no intention of progressing construction, other than some initial clearance, until planning permission is granted that would protect Sport England's interests and ensure the sports facilities that the community want, will be built."

Tim Hollingsworth, Chief Executive of Sport England said in a letter to local MP Maria Miller: "Until this agreement and the club's needs are satisfied Sport England will continue to maintain our objection to planning proposals on the

Camrose site and seek to secure mitigation for the loss of playing fields at Camrose Stadium."

Basingstoke Town football manager Dan Brownlie spoke out by showing his frustration at the ongoing scandal. Brownlie had previously been co-manager at Hartley Wintney helping guide them to considerable success.

DAN BROWNLIE – LEFT – BASINGSTOKE TOWN
MANAGER

I've been involved in the Football Club under a couple of different positions for two years now. I am buoyed by the idea, ambition and execution of getting Basingstoke back to where it belongs, and I am excited about the potential future of this great club.

A club I am truly proud to manage and represent – and whilst it's arguably unusual for management to involve themselves in off-field matters like this; like anything – I can't moan about its result if I am unprepared to put at least my voice towards it. Whilst the club are working tirelessly to take this club forward; across no-man's land is a fighter jet in the name of Rafi Razzak, camping in the other direction.

Just by way of introduction – I see reason before I see doubt; and despite forceful narratives I will attempt to take each person with as open mind as possible. With that in mind, as I hadn't been hugely immersed in the goings on of the Camrose fiasco – I along with Kevin White (Vice-Chairman) took the time to go and visit Rafi in his offices in a bid to get a greater understanding. Terry had previously attempted these conversations; but understandably he got quite heated with the ignorance.

In the same meeting I also met Malcolm McPhail who, to confirm in case you were in any doubt, he has absolutely no interest in the community he is destroying at the club and was purely interested in numbers. Their numbers.

Needless to say, the thinly veiled attempts at appearing interested in the club and its survival; the empty promises and his unwavering belief that what he was doing is completely ethical was quite startling but not surprising. I guess living by the adage of "if you tell a lie big enough and keep repeating it, people will eventually come to believe it" also applied to his own self-belief. The historians amongst you will forgive me for not naming where that quote derives from, although… no. No, I'll leave that there.

Humour me if you can, just for a moment… Let's put aside the fact that over the course of the past ten years, The Camrose was left to rot. On one occasion, Martin Kuhl did a team talk in complete darkness with only him lit up by the torch on my iPhone – two weeks after the electric went in the changing rooms.

Let's put aside the fact he overturned a 100-year covenant put in place by Lord Camrose and his gift to the community. Put aside the fact he now plans to sell the land protected land to line his own pockets. Put aside the fact he evicted a club from its own home.

Put aside the fact he actioned the digging up of the Camrose pitch without planning application and in a bid to cover up the findings claimed he was reseeding it (for anyone that has been down there recently… not much grass coming through.) Put aside the fact that he began selling items that were gifted by the community on eBay. Let's put aside the fact on numerous occasions that he has claimed to not let the club die.

CHAPTER 32

HAMPSHIRE IS A WONDERFUL COUNTY – SHAME ABOUT THE COUNCIL

WINCHESTER CATHEDRAL

It was in 1973 when I moved to Basingstoke shortly after getting married to Sue. The attraction was cheaper housing than that which was available in Slough where we lived. I did not expect to stay too long and envisaged moving back towards London where I had undertaken most of my work previously. However, here we are 47 years later and still here.

I have always thought that somehow Basingstoke could have been developed better once it was announced that it was going to be an overspill town for London. In my opinion the town lacks a main feature. By that I mean either a river or being near the sea. However, I recognise it as home and one thing it has, is many truly smashing people. From arriving in the town I have always felt welcome and in particular the 'original' Stokies.

Not too far from Basingstoke we have some beautiful countryside and small towns. Arlesford is one of my favourites. I have always been fascinated by the Alton to Basingstoke light railway which finished in 1936. The restored Watercress line from Arlesford to Alton is popular and we take the occasional trip on it.

Hampshire County Council are based in Winchester and when I started up my business in the early 1990s they were to become one of my first customers. They contacted me when they found out that I had left my previous employer and asked if I wanted work. For around five years this was an absolute delight. The work was breakdowns, repairs and very small projects in Libraries, Schools, Colleges, Libraries and Care Homes etc. This involved visiting some of the wonderful parts of the County. From the New Forest to Church Crookham. From Southsea to Lymington. From Tadley to Ringwood. Having been in a very pressured job which could be stressful, this was heaven on earth. In my opinion Hampshire is a wonderful county with wonderful people. Second only to Govan, of course, where I hail from!!

The end of our work with Hampshire County Council came about when they effectively closed their inside Estates Department where we got our work from. This was given to sizable outside Contractors who were more difficult to deal with. Most especially getting paid in a reasonable time scale. We had our biggest ever dent to our cash flow when the main contractor on a Hampshire County Council contract went bust. This cost us a lot of money from a Contractor called Johnson and Baxter who were on the Hampshire County Council's approved suppliers list. The name of Hampshire County Council entered the Camrose Scandal in recent times by giving Basron a lifeline in their bid for development of the Camrose ground. They approved the completely unneeded Link Road through the ground. This decision has sparked outrage in the town coupled with another ill thought decision to close a busy road into Basingstoke at Chapel Hill. This was overturned after mass objections.

Rob Humby's intervention:

A MULTI-MILLION pound scheme to build a new road in Hampshire has been given the green light.

Cllr Rob Humby, executive member for economy, transport and environment at Hampshire County Council, has backed plans to build a new road through the Camrose ground in Basingstoke. The so-called Camrose Link Road would be a 240m long single carriageway link between the A30 Winchester Road and Western Way.

It will be partially built across land previously used by Basingstoke Football Club for its football pitch.

The plans also include proposals for a signalised junction with the A30 Winchester Road with pedestrian and cycle crossings as well as the closure of the Western Way exit onto Brighton Hill roundabout.

However, Cllr Humby's decision will now be subject to the outcome of separate plans for a 70-bedroom care home and 89 new homes at the Camrose site.

The news comes as Sport England and Basingstoke and Deane Borough Council have raised an objection to the Camrose Link Road plans due to loss of the sports facilities.

The county council said the full details for providing suitable alternative sports facilities for the Camrose football ground are being agreed.

At the meeting held this afternoon, Cllr Humby also gave the green light to plans for a compulsory purchase order to buy the land required to deliver the scheme.

Talking to members about the proposals he said: " What this enables us to do is to progress with the overall scheme, acknowledging that this is in partnership with Basingstoke and Deane council as well and we know that some of that is dependent on planning permission. I am pleased to see this and to see that we are progressing. I am very happy to accept the recommendations."

Official documents revealed that the link road planning application is expected to be considered by the county council's Regulatory Committee on July 29 2020.

Meanwhile, Basingstoke and Deane Borough Council is expected to consider the plans for a care home and new homes at the Camrose site in September this year.

The county council said the Camrose Link Road Scheme will unlock land for business and residential developments on the Camrose site and will advantage the operation of Brighton Hill roundabout.

The authority also said the Camrose Link Road forms "a key component" of the proposed £20 million Brighton Hill improvements which would provide an alternative route between Western Way and the A30.

At today's meeting Cllr Humby also approved plans for advanced enabling works at the Brighton Hill roundabout.

Humby seemed to be in dispute around the County with his efforts to help Developers. At Gosport and Fareham a dispute arose when permission was given to build on land that was designated as separating Gosport from Fareham. With the Development they would effectively be joined together. The same Councillor was forced to stand down from Winchester Council over his actions on the Silver Hill Development. News extract below.

Winchester Silver Hill: Leader Robert Humby stands down

17 February 2015

The leader of a council responsible for "unlawful" decisions over a £165m shopping development is stepping down.

Conservative leader of Winchester City Council Robert Humby said he "must take responsibility" for the High Court judgement over Silver Hill.

The Liberal Democrat group had been planning to put forward a motion of no confidence in the leader on Thursday's full council meeting.

The High Court ruled decisions relating to the city centre plans were unlawful.

A judge said the council had acted unlawfully on 11 February by allowing the developer to revise the Silver Hill plans without putting the scheme back out to commercial tender.

Mr Humby said at the time: "I won't stand down. As leader of the council my job is to lead the council through this difficult process."

'Badly wrong'

In a statement on Tuesday he said: "I stand by the decisions I and the cabinet made on Silver Hill.

Winchester Silver Hill: Leader Robert Humby stands down - BBC News

"Nevertheless, I was leader when the court decision was handed down and so must take responsibility for that judgement.

"The decisions on Silver Hill were taken after consulting with officers and taking external legal advice."

Liberal Democrat Martin Tod said: "It was the right thing for him to resign. Things have been going badly wrong.

"It is not just down to him things have gone wrong and we wanted to change the administration."

The Conservatives have 28 seats on the council, Liberal Democrats have 25, Labour has three and there is one Independent councillor.

The Department for Communities and Local Government spokesman said it is considering whether to call-in the planning case.

The department has issued a direction which means all action must be frozen on the application.

"The decisions on Silver Hill were taken after consulting with officers and taking external legal advice."

Liberal Democrat Martin Tod said: "It was the right thing for him to resign. Things have been going badly wrong.

"It is not just down to him things have gone wrong and we wanted to change the administration."

The Conservatives have 28 seats on the council, Liberal Democrats have 25, Labour has three and there is one Independent councillor.

The Department for Communities and Local Government spokesman said it is considering whether to call-in the planning case.

The department has issued a direction which means all action must be frozen on the application.

The scandal took another twist with excellent research from Ryan Evans at the Gazette and revelations regarding the shares. Dave Stratton was the most popular supporter the club had and he sadly passed away during summer 2019. Dave Stratton's widow bravely contacted the Gazette and told of the shabby way in which the Shareholders were treated.

MANDY STRATTON WITH DAVE STRATTON (ADJACENT)

TWO LIFE-LONG Basingstoke Town Football Club supporters were allegedly pressured into selling their shares in the club to **Rafi Razzak.**

Mandy Stratton says that she and her late husband, David, had a knock on the door out of the blue in 2016, from a man who gave them a cheque and said that he was going to be buying their share in Basingstoke Town Ltd, the company that ran the club. Mr Razzak has denied this.

*She has decided to speak out after the **Gazette** exclusively revealed last week that the existence of a preferential share could have given fans a chance to block the club's eviction from the Camrose.*

Soon Mandy Stratton was followed by long-time popular club member Jim Gould who claimed he had been duped. Gazette article:

BASINGSTOKE football fans were "duped" into selling their stake in the club after being told their shares were worthless, it has been claimed.

Former owner of Basingstoke Town Football Club has been accused of telling shareholders their shares wasn't worth anything before he struck a multi-million pound deal for the freehold of the Camrose football ground.

*Documents seen by The **Gazette** reveal that in May 2016, the former football club owner wrote to all shareholders informing them that the club was "unviable", his "support will not continue beyond the short term", and that their shares had "no value".*

He then subsequently offered to re-purchase their shares, explaining it was to ensure that [the fans] were not "out of pocket".

Three years previous, Jim Gould answered queries in respect to the Preferential Share on a Fans Forum.

jimgould
Full Member
★★★
Mar 16, 2017 at 3:06pm
hoody84 likes this

Quote

Jack, the people I dealt with purchased shares under the "The Friends of BTFC" umbrella and were given their surrender cheques along with the reason personally by me with the exception of 3 people, one of those being deceased.

Re - the "Golden Share", rumours exist but from paper work that I have cannot pin point where it landed.
I was instructed to liaise with Phillips the solicitors over surrendering the shares perhaps they can help or the Companies House web site relating to the shares issue may shed a light.

Apologises for delay in responding.

RYAN EVANS –

BASINGSTOKE GAZETTE

The definition of a Scandal is:

A scandal is a very public incident which involves a claim of wrong-doing, shame, or moral offence.

RAFI RAZZAK (CENTRE)

The central figure in the Camrose Scandal is of course Rafi Razzak. It is true that Malcolm McPhail at Basron, David Knight at Basingstoke Town Ltd and Phillips the Solicitors gave assistance to help him achieve his ambitions. However, Razzak bears the responsibility for the appalling sequence of events that have led a town's football club to lose its ground.

The Community Club set themselves the goal of getting to Winklebury in 2017. This of course was a mitigation. It never could be a replacement for the Camrose. Until recently they seemed to find it difficult to embrace the two-stadium solution. Indeed neither the Chairman Terry Brown nor the Deputy Chairman Kevin White spoke at the February 2020 Council meeting. However, with the 'History is Watching' slogan, it has to be hoped that they themselves will be part of a positive history.

Basingstoke Councillors mostly appear blissfully unaware that they are dealing with a full-blown scandal. Hence they have not come up with the Replacement Ground for the Camrose. Parrott fashion we hear, 'Mr Razzak is both sides of the Covenant. Therefore there is nothing we can do about it!' If Razzak is both sides of the argument then it is a 'Conflict of Interests' which requires careful scrutiny. It is difficult to imagine any other Council in the country handle this scandal as badly as Basingstoke Council.

It was been one year exactly since my week in politics. However, out of the blue I was invited to a meeting with Ken Rhatagan, the Leader of Basingstoke Council. This transpired when I quoted on Social Media a post relating to Councillors getting a pay rise. I mentioned that I could not get the Councillors to do anything or even meet with me. The meeting went very much as I expected. Ken Rhatagan came across as a decent guy. However, we are poles apart on the way forward. Ken wants Winklebury and I want a new or upgraded replacement for the Camrose.

The saga continues and will re-start when Council meetings resume in September 2020. The scandal, the worst ever in non-league football, has shown that the Council appear to have gone to great lengths to try and gain approval for the Basron Development plans against the wishes of the Basingstoke people.

For me it is the end of the road. It has been a year since I got involved in applying pressure to try and get the situation resolved. Age and health mean I have to consider what I have to get involved in. Sue and the family are urging me to give it up, thinking it is a thankless task. They are of course right. As an author I have used the coronavirus lockdown to write this book. It has given me some enjoyment and I hope it will also provide readers with some interest, enjoyment and an insight into the worst scandal in non-league football. It serves as a warning to any football clubs looking to a wealthy benefactor to help them with financial difficulties.

HOW WILL IT FINISH?

ANYONE'S GUESS, IN MY OPINION.

THE BASINGSTOKE PEOPLE DESERVE FAR BETTER

THAN THIS.

ABOUT THE AUTHOR

David Graham is a 72 year old retired Control System Engineer. Born in the Govan district of Glasgow he attended Drumoyne Primary School until 12 years of age. Moved to Govan High School and left the school in 1963 with no qualifications.

Moved to Slough and obtained a 5-year-electrical apprenticeship at Satchwell Control Systems. Continued at the company as a Service Engineer before moving to the Churchill Hotel in London. After a year moved on to Johnson Controls as a Service and Commissioning Engineer. Then followed employment at Staefa Controls for a period of 16 years. During this period the author started as Commissioning Engineer and then Commissioning and Service Manager for 9 years. On leaving Staefa Controls set up Basingstoke Control Systems as a small family business. This continued for 24 years until full retirement a few years ago. Family members Sue, Stuart and Matt were employed in the small enterprise and I am indebted to their efforts.

A lifelong football enthusiast starting with Rangers and the local Non League side Benburb in Govan. Supported Slough Town when living in the town before moving to Basingstoke in 1973. Followed the fortunes of Basingstoke Town and also some of the other local football teams. Now supports and helps Hartley Wintney FC an excellent club in every respect. Writes match reports for Hartley Wintney which appear in the Basingstoke Gazette, Basingstoke Observer, the Non League Paper as well as Farnborough and Aldrshot papers plus others.

As an author has written much on Scotland especially around Loch Lomand and the Trossachs with short articles. In 2014 was author of 'A Time in Govan'. A book about Govan 1945 to 1963.

INDEX